Amgueddfa Cymru
National Mu

Wales celebrating the first 100 years

First published in 2007 by National Museum Wales Books,
Cathays Park, Cardiff CF10 3NP Wales.

ISBN 978-0-7200-0583-7

Editing and production: Rebecca Brumbill, Jo Collins, Mari Gordon, Kay Kays and Phil Smith.
Design: Peter Gill & Associates

national museum wales
amgueddfa cymru

Sponsored by
Welsh Assembly
Government

Images on facing page from left to right, Sir Mortimer Wheeler (1890-1976), *Midday, L'Estaque* (1878-80) by Paul Cézanne and detail of St Catherine's face from St Teilo's Church.

Amgueddfa Cymru National Museum Wales celebrating the first 100 years

Making sense of the world

As we present this book in celebration of Amgueddfa Cymru – National Museum Wales in this, our centenary, year, the world is a very different place to that which saw the creation of the Museum in 1907.

Over these last one hundred years the Museum has borne witness to remarkable events on a local and global scale: two world wars, the decline of the 'traditional' heavy industries of Wales, the rise of the new technologies, the devolution of Welsh government, natural disasters across the globe, and events closer to home, such as the Aberfan disaster of 1966, that have united our visitors in their quest to make sense of the world that surrounds them.

Throughout this time and amid these many changes, the mission of the Museum has remained remarkably constant. It is our aim to present the national collections of art, archaeology, industry, natural history and social history in ways that open pathways of understanding for our visitors so that the objects, so richly illustrated in this book, tell their own unique stories, illuminating the past and opening up a myriad of possible futures – for the next hundred years and beyond.

Michael Houlihan
Director General

Acknowledgments

Amgueddfa Cymru – National Museum Wales has always relied on funding from a wide range of sources. Our fine buildings were built as a result of public donations and some of our most famous collections were generously given to us by benefactors. Over the last hundred years, the Museum has been fortunate to receive grants and funding from a number of organizations, businesses, individuals and charitable trusts and foundations too numerous to list.

More recently, projects you will read about in this book have been funded by The Aggregates Levy Sustainability Fund, The Art Fund, Barclays plc, Coalfields Regeneration Trust, The Derek Williams Trust, The European Structural Funds ERDF Objective One Programme, The Friends of the National Museum of Wales, The Garfield Weston Foundation, The GC Gibson Charitable Trust, The Goldsmiths' Company, The Headley Trust, Heritage Lottery Fund, The Lloyds TSB Foundation for England and Wales, Local Regeneration Fund, Patrons of Amgueddfa Cymru – National Museum Wales, The Wales Tourist Board, The Welsh Assembly Government, The Welsh Development Agency and The Wolfson Foundation.

Contents

Foreword by Michael Houlihan, Director General v

1907 - 1917 4

1917 - 1927 22

1927 - 1937 38

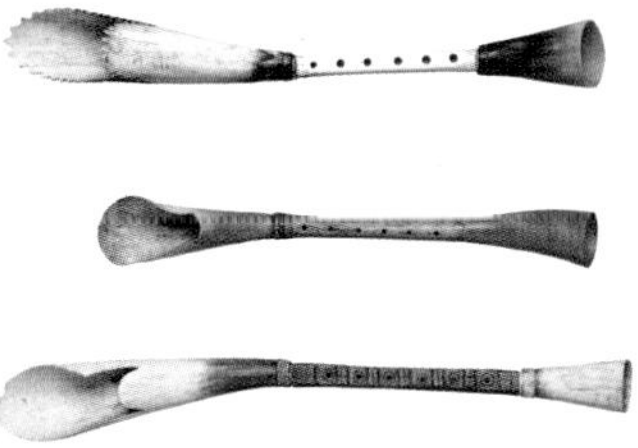

1937 - 1947 48

1947 - 1957 66

1957 - 1967 86

1967 - 1977 96

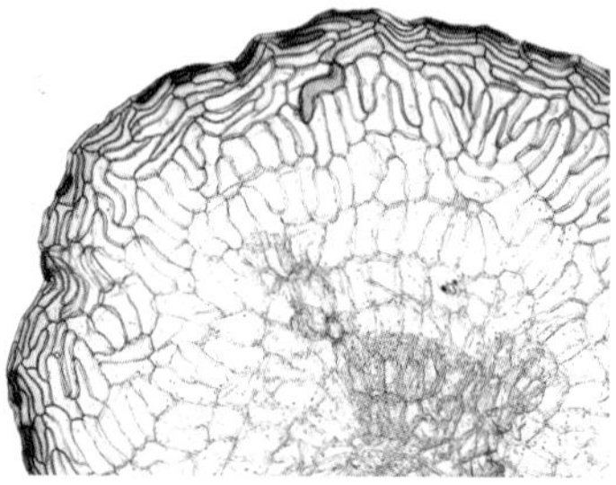

1977 - 1987 114

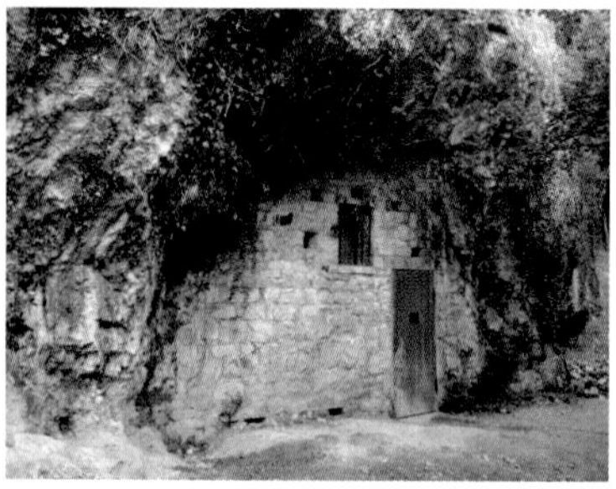
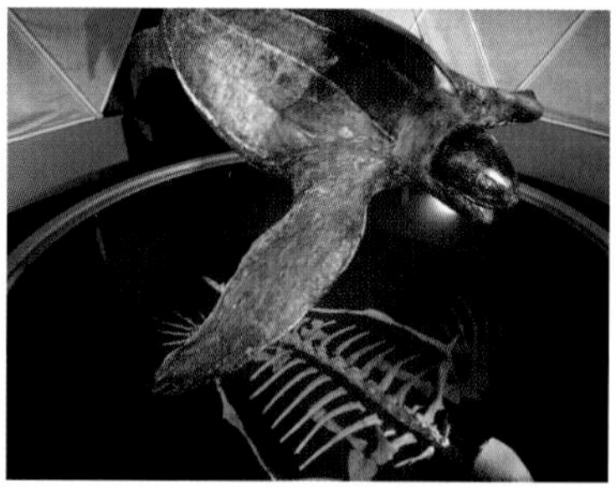

1987 - 1997 130

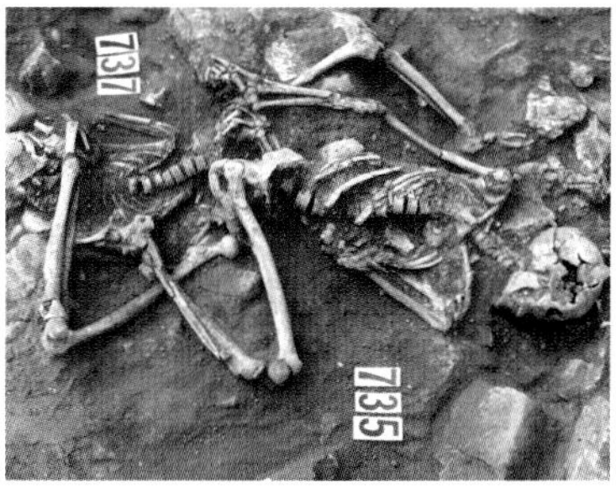

1997 - 2007 148

Current and future developments 174

Interesting facts and figures 176

Information on the seven museums 178

General information 180

List of directors 182

Further reading 183

Index 184

1907 - 1917

The birth of a national institution.

The National Museum of Wales was incorporated by a Royal Charter, granted on 19 March 1907.

The Museum's inception dates from the 1880s when there was a movement in Wales towards the establishment of national institutions. Out of this flourish of Victorian and Edwardian nationalism also grew the University of Wales in 1893 and the National Library, incorporated on the same day as the Museum.

The founders of the Museum wanted to create a body that represented all the chief interests in Wales – educational, industrial and political – and the Charter of 1907 based the concept of a Court of Governors on that already established for the University of Wales. This Court originally included all Welsh MPs and representatives from all county councils and county boroughs.

The Charter makes it clear that the Museum's first aim was to collect, study, care for and present the material culture and natural heritage of Wales. Contemporary commentators were clear that this geographical focus made it different from the principal national museums and galleries in London, most of which had an international, even global, role.

The Museum's stated object was 'mainly and primarily the complete illustration of the geology, mineralogy, zoology, botany, ethnography, archaeology, art history and special industries of Wales and the collection, preservation and maintenance of objects and things of usefulness or interested connected therewith.'

Its Seal was described thus: 'Within a circle of two and a half inches diameter, a symbolic figure of "Learning" is seated upon a fragment of architecture, holding in her right hand a tablet upon which is shewn the badge of Wales, namely a Dragon. In the background are some Ionic columns and entablature. On the right-hand side of the seated figures appears the wording Seal of the National Museum of Wales, and on the left-hand side Sêl Amgueddfa Genedlaethol Cymru.'

The Museum's first mission statement was created by Lord Pontypridd, the Museum's first President, in 1912: 'to teach the world about Wales and … the Welsh people about their own Fatherland.' Its more formal expression in the Charter emphasized that the Museum was being instituted 'for the benefit of the education of the Public'.

Above and right: The seal of the new National Museum of Wales, designed by Sir William Goscombe John.

SÊL AMGVEDDFA
GENEDLAETHOL
CYMRV

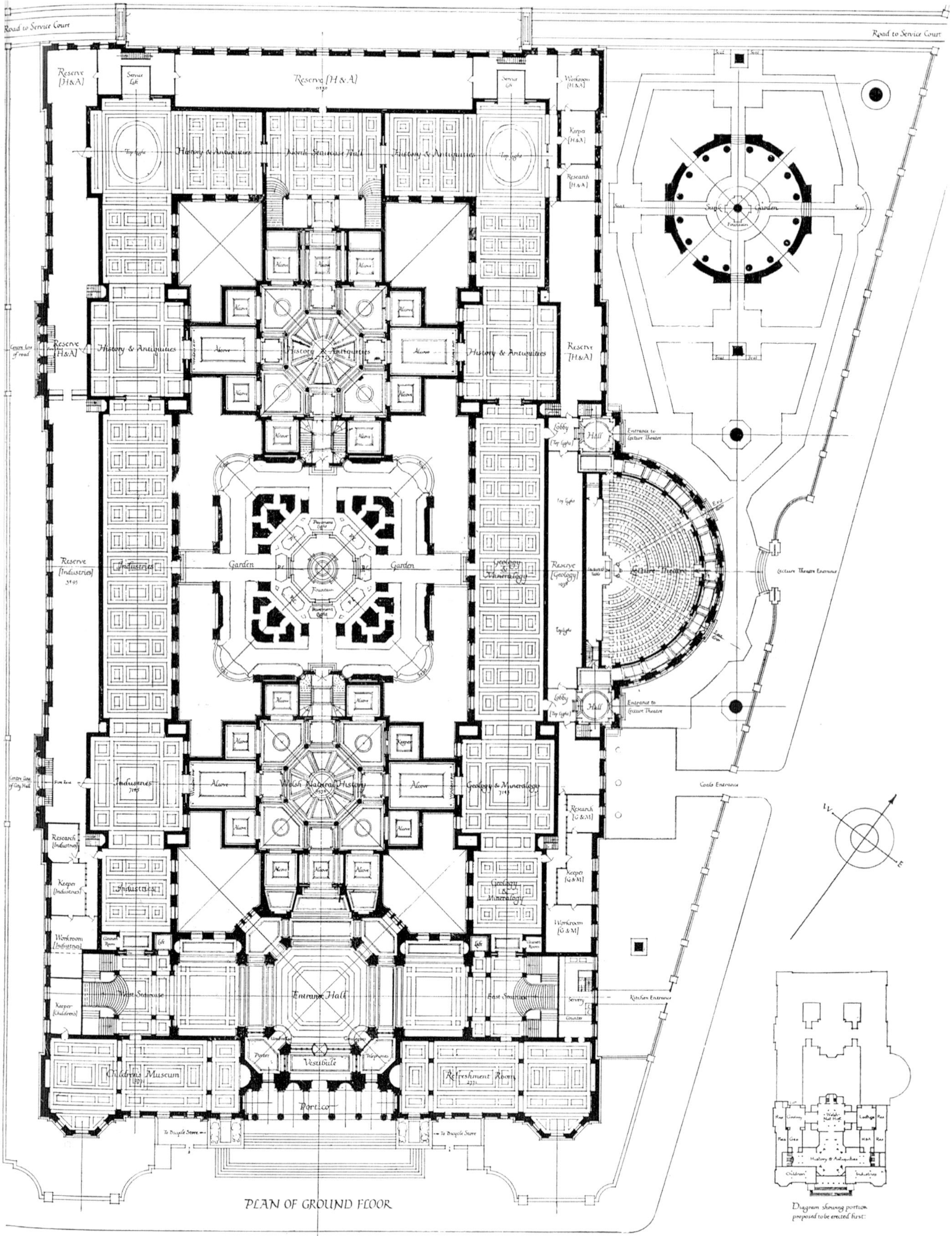
Road to Service Court
Road to Service Court
Reserve [H&A]
Service Lift
Reserve [H&A]
Workroom [H&A]
History & Antiquities
North Staircase Hall
History & Antiquities
Keeper [H&A]
Research [H&A]
Sunk Garden
Alcove
History & Antiquities
Reserve [H&A]
Entrance to Lecture Theatre
Lobby
Hall
Garden
Fountain
Garden
Reserve [Industries]
Industries
Geology & Mineralogy
Reserve [Geology]
Lecture Theatre
Lecture Theatre Entrance
Welsh Natural History
Industries
Geology & Mineralogy
Coals Entrance
Research [G & M]
Research [Industries]
Keeper [Industries]
Keeper [G & M]
Workroom [G & M]
Workroom [Industries]
West Staircase
Entrance Hall
East Staircase
Kitchen Entrance
Keeper [Children]
Vestibule
Porter
Telephones
Children's Museum
Refreshment Room
Portico
To Bicycle Store
To Bicycle Store
PLAN OF GROUND FLOOR
Diagram showing portion proposed to be erected first.

A special competition produces a winner and a new museum for Wales.

The progress from 1907's granting of the Royal Charter to the laying of the Museum's foundation stone five years later was steady. One of the most important developments during this time was the hosting of an open architectural competition. The winning entrant would have the life-altering chance to design the new museum's permanent home.

In 1909, Arnold Dunbar Smith and partner Cecil Claude Brewer came first in the architectural competition to design the Museum's new home.

Dunbar Smith was born in Islington in 1866, entered the Royal Academy Schools in 1890 and formed a partnership with Brewer in 1895.

Brewer (1871-1918) also studied at the Royal Academy Schools from 1893 to 1898, and it was at this time that he met Smith. Both architects were members of the Art Workers Guild (Brewer was elected in 1901, Smith in 1922), which provided a forum for ideas and encouraged co-operation between architects, artists and craftsmen. Brewer also served on the Art Workers Guild Committee from 1906 to 1907 and was a founding leader of the Design and Industries Association.

Until they won the chance to design the National Museum of Wales, Smith and Brewer had designed mainly domestic creations using vernacular traditions. The monumental national museum building was one of the earliest in Great Britain to use the Beaux-Arts style then popular in the United States, at a time when architects were returning to classicism, particularly for large, public buildings.

Left: The ground floor plan as envisaged in the winning design. Above: Elevation from the south west from the winning design by Dunbar Smith and Brewer.

The Museum receives its first exhibits.

On 15 November 1912, Alderman Morgan Thomas, the Lord Mayor of Cardiff, handed over a deed of covenant to Lord Pontypridd, President of the youthful National Museum of Wales. The deed transferred the contents of Cardiff's Municipal Museum to the new institution.

Until the 1880s, the Municipal Museum was essentially a museum of natural history, with a geological collection as its chief feature. In its range it was essentially British, although the palaeontology of south Wales was well represented. However, much was stored in boxes and drawers due to the lack of proper museum accommodation.

Another attractive exhibit was a collection of Wales's wild birds. This had been mainly formed by Honorary Curator Mr T. W. Proger. More natural delights were inherited by the new museum in the form of a herbarium featuring more than 3,500 plant specimens.

It wasn't all about natural treasures, however. Back in 1882 the loan of the valuable Menelaus Collection of oil paintings had laid the foundation of the Municipal Museum's art exhibits. Pictures and sculptures were then gradually acquired and, in 1897, the executors of wealthy corn merchant James Pyke Thompson's estate donated many watercolours. Additionally, the largest and most representative collection of Welsh porcelain and earthenware of the time had also been amassed by the time all its objects were transferred.

Long before the 1912 handover, the Municipal Museum had become highly regarded among other provincial museums because of the rapid growth of its archaeological collections. The prehistoric collection was largely Welsh, its most notable feature being a series of Iron Age bronzes. In 1894, the Museum committee decided to form a complete collection of casts of Wales's sculptured and inscribed pre-Norman stones. The collection was unique, and is still of great value; no other country had made a similar attempt to represent all its monuments of any particular period, and it was a fitting bequest for the new national museum.

The collections of the Municipal Museum, known as the 'Cardiff Collections', were considerable and several were of recognised importance. This museum may have gone – but its fine legacy lives on.

Right: Inside Cardiff's Municipal Museum.

Near the start of a brilliant career, JMW Turner studies a jewel in the Vale of Glamorgan crown.

Joseph Mallord William Turner (1775-1851) was one of Britain's most visionary artists. A Londoner, he gleaned much early inspiration from Wales, as illustrated by his *Transept of Ewenny Priory, Glamorganshire,* completed in around 1797.

The priory church of St Michael in Ewenny, near Bridgend, dates back to 1115-1120 when it was founded by Lord of Ogmore William de Londres for the Benedictine community.

Almost seven centuries later, in 1795, Turner visited the Priory. Only twenty years old, Turner had already been admitted to the Royal Academy Schools and had publicly exhibited watercolours.

His journey to Ewenny was part of a tour of south Wales. He took notes and made a pencil sketch of the site, later creating this highly finished exhibition watercolour. It depicts a dramatic view across the Priory's south transept.

The work was shown at the Royal Academy in 1797, where it moved a reviewer to write: 'In point of colour and effect this is one of the grandest drawings we have ever seen, and equal to the best pictures of Rembrandt.'

The figure of a knight on the altar tomb at the right of the picture is probably Sir Paganus de Turberville of Coity, a twelfth-century benefactor of the Priory.

Turner enjoyed visiting Wales several times over the first ten years of his career. The country provided the inspiration for some of his most intense and romantic watercolours.

Widely recognized as one of Britain's great landscape artists, he began with watercolours and copper plate engravings known as mezzotints. In 1799 he was elected an Associate of the Royal Academy, becoming a full member three years later. By then he was acknowledged to be one of Britain's leading watercolourists.

A prolific artist, he travelled extensively in the British Isles and on the Continent. He was especially renowned for his dynamic treatment of natural light effects in land and seascapes. Today, we recognize the direct influence of his work on the development of Impressionism.

Amgueddfa Cymru – National Museum Wales acquired this work with the rest of the collections that came from the Municipal Museum in 1912.

Left and above: *Transept of Ewenny Priory, Glamorganshire* (c.1797) by J M W Turner.

Daring expeditions lead to a treasured study of sea life.

World travel was far from comfortable in the Victorian era. But this didn't stand in the way of many adventurous crews who sailed to some of the world's most extreme locations and returned with an astonishing range of previously undiscovered creatures. The Museum's first director, mollusc expert W. Evans Hoyle, was one of the main beneficiaries.

Left, above and right: Original cephalopod specimens from W. Evans Hoyle's collection.

Squid, octopus and cuttlefish are members of a class of mollusc called Cephalopoda. One major difference to other molluscs is the presence of tentacles that surround the head. W. Evans Hoyle (1855-1926) was fascinated by them, and built up an important body of work on the subject. Material from his major studies between 1883 and 1912 now form the backbone of the Museum's cephalopod collection.

Hoyle is most famous for his scholarly writing on cephalopods brought back by major expeditions of his era, notably the *Challenger*, the *Albatross*, the British National Antarctic Expedition and the Scottish National Antarctic Expedition.

He also studied material collected by William A. Herdman from the Gulf of Manaar in the Indian Ocean, Cyril Crossland from Zanzibar and Stanley Gardner from the Maldives and Laccadives off India.

Trained as a medical anatomist, his cephalopod studies exhibit his skill in fine dissection. He wrote a number of papers on cephalopod structure and was responsible for comprehensive catalogues of Cephalopoda in 1886 and 1909.

The Museum's identification of the cephalopods remains as it was when Hoyle acquired the collection. A meticulous researcher, he retained many of his manuscript papers, including original line illustrations. Typical of this material is the first proof of his 1885 paper on *Loligopsis*, extensively annotated by Professor of Zoology Japetus Steenstrup and accompanied by a hand-written letter from Steenstrup dated January 1885.

Like many colleagues, he collected ephemera related to the subject, and the collection includes letters from other cephalopod researchers. He also amassed a library on cephalopods, which was augmented later by a 1955 bequest from John Read le Brockton Tomlin.

National Museum
Cephalopoda
Polypus
det.W.E.H. leg.
Naples
HOYLE No

FE 22-1-1
HERBARIUM, NATIONAL MUSEUM OF WALES (NMW)
FLORA OF MONS.
POLYPODIUM CAMBRICUM L.
Locality Railway cutting nr quarry (disused)
CHEPSTOW
High up behind
Collector G. HUTCHINSON
V.C. 35
Map/Grid Ref. 31/537929
Date 17.2.1990
Reg. No. V91.104.42

An important plant collection is taken over by the newly constituted National Museum of Wales.

Vascular plants comprise the general groupings of ferns, conifers and flowering plants. They form the dominant vegetation through most of the world. The Museum's Vascular Plant Herbarium is a collection that aims to give a complete illustration of the flora of Wales. To enable the flora to be put into context, there is also material from Europe and the rest of the world. The collection is international in scope, importance and quality.

This collection originated in 1870 when the Municipal Museum bought some dried plants brought together in the 1830s by Charles Conway. The collection was added to over the years by individual collectors. By 1912, the collection had around 3,500 mounted specimens and was taken over by the newly constituted National Museum of Wales.

Today, the Herbarium has more than 240,000 specimens. Around half the contents are of Welsh origin, a quarter from the rest of the British Isles, twenty-two per cent foreign and three per cent cultivated. Virtually all native British plants are represented, as well as many introduced species. There are more than 380 type specimens (specimens by which others are identified).

The Herbarium is an essential reference resource for botanists and is well used by the public.

Left: A specimen of *Polypodium cambricum* L.
Above: The two sori of *Polypodium cambricum* L.

Building starts on a fitting home for Wales's national museum.

The building now known as National Museum Cardiff is part of the mainly Edwardian civic complex of Cathays Park, in Cardiff's city centre. This was Britain's first intentionally planned civic centre. The site now includes, among others, the City Hall, law courts and university and Welsh Assembly Government buildings. It was deemed to be an appropriate setting for the fledgling National Museum of Wales.

The original plan for a purpose-built home for the young National Museum of Wales showed a long rectangular structure with a large central courtyard and central garden. Its external appearance was designed to be in harmony with the neighbouring City Hall.

The first contract for the building was let in 1911, and the following year King George V laid the foundation stone. The collections of the then Cardiff Municipal Museum were transferred to the new national museum.

During the First World War, building operations were suspended, and it was not until 1926 that the existing superstructure was completed. The King returned to formally open the Museum on 21 April 1927.

In 1993, there was another Royal unveiling, as Queen Elizabeth II opened the new Courtyard Galleries extension.

Right: The laying of the foundation stone of the new building in 1912 by King George V.

THIS FOUNDATION STONE WAS LAID BY
HIS MAJESTY KING GEORGE V
ON THE 26th DAY OF JUNE 1912 A.D.

An exhibition takes place – in a borrowed gallery.

Above: The *Loans Exhibition* at Cardiff's City Hall.

Thanks to Cardiff's City Hall and the generosity of dedicated benefactors, the Museum managed to exhibit key works – despite having not yet been built.

Before the opening of its purpose-built home at Cathays Park in 1927, the Museum made full use of a gallery in the neighbouring City Hall. It had been specifically built for temporary exhibitions, and hosted the famous *Loans Exhibition* of 1913.

This exhibition featured pieces of art loaned by Welsh philanthropists Gwendoline and Margaret Davies from their extensive and pioneering collections. It was a reflection of their desire to raise the standing of the visual arts in Wales. Later, the sisters would become major benefactors to the Museum.

One feature of the *Loans Exhibition* was a bronze of Rodin's *The Kiss*, bought by Gwendoline in Paris in 1912, and a major highlight of the exhibition.

Thomas Henry Thomas brings together Wales's sciences and arts.

More than 1,000 prints, drawings and watercolours came to the Museum in the early twentieth century as a series of gifts and, following Thomas Henry Thomas's death in 1915, two further large bequests followed. They are exceptionally wide-ranging, including the depiction of modern rural and industrial life, the natural world, archaeology, anthropological and ethnographical drawings, geology, book illustration and folklore.

After training as an artist at Carey's school in London and at the Royal Academy, Thomas Henry Thomas spent time in France and Italy. On his return to London in 1864, he devoted himself to portraiture, design and book illustration. He worked as a special artist for *The Graphic* and *The Daily Graphic*. His Welsh heritage was of great importance to him, and he became involved with the *Eisteddfod* and the *Gorsedd*. He joined the Royal Cambrian Academy and was a key member, and president, of the Cardiff Naturalists' Society. Many of his illustrations were for this society.

He accompanied scientific expeditions, including a trip to the west coast of Ireland to study ocean fauna, an area of research that continues in the Museum's Department of Biodiversity and Systematic Biology to this day. His interest in geology led him to study the volcanoes of Sicily and the Neapolitan district. Back in Wales, near Porthcawl, he discovered a large stone slab in the churchyard of Newton Nottage. Recognized as a significant find, it was named *Brontozoum thomasii* as a tribute – and was the first dinosaur footprint found in Wales.

The strength of the Thomas collection lies in its quirkiness, its breadth, and the fact that it encompasses most of the major concerns of the nineteenth century. Thomas can be viewed in the tradition of J. W. Goethe and John Ruskin, men whose works spanned many diverse disciplines and sought to bridge the gap between science and the arts. Today, Thomas is seen as one of the founding fathers of the National Museum of Wales.

Left: Two of T. H. Thomas's mining paintings.
Above: Portrait of T. H. Thomas by Christopher Williams.

1917 - 1927

Right: A Meissen coffee pot, c. 1715-20, donated by de Winton in 1918.
Far right: Wilfred de Winton.

A Welsh enthusiast illuminates porcelain's colourful European history.

Wilfred de Winton (1856-1929), from a prosperous Breconshire banking family, was a major benefactor of the Museum. He donated more than 3,000 pieces of European porcelain from the eighteenth and early nineteenth centuries, which form one of the most important such collections in any British museum.

Europe took time to catch up with the Far East when it came to producing true porcelain. This white translucent material originated in China, from where it was shipped westwards in huge quantities. Japan had begun producing it in the 1600s but the nearest European imitation of that century was an artificial French variety.

In 1709 the secret of making true porcelain was discovered in Europe by alchemist Johann Friedrich Böttger. The first European porcelain factory was founded in 1710 by Augustus the Strong, ruler of the German state of Saxony, in the town of Meissen. Others were established throughout Germany, supported by princes who wanted the prestige that these factories brought, and in Vienna.

Early European porcelain was of great interest to Wilfred de Winton when he began collecting in the 1890s. The collection is rich in Böttger's earliest porcelain and numerous painted and enamelled wares covering typical styles of Meissen decoration, such as underglaze blue and Kakiemon styles inspired by China and Japan.

The Meissen factory's heyday was over by the mid-1750s and its later wares were not popular with early collectors, although the de Winton collection does contain examples.

A treasured natural history collection is acquired by the Museum.

A minor composer of songs and piano music he might have been – and an author of books, a poet and an amateur artist; but Robert Henry Fernando Rippon is best remembered for privately publishing the first specialist book on birdwing butterflies. Titled *Icones Ornithopterorum*, each copy contained 111 beautifully hand-coloured prints. However, this accomplished gentleman also left the Museum another fine legacy.

Rippon was born in Essex in 1836. From boyhood he took great delight in natural history.

His collection of insects was developed over forty years of assiduous labour. It contained material from most parts of the world, notably Central and South America, South-East Asia and South Africa. The collection also had material from other collectors, including Charles Darwin. It eventually comprised 105,765 specimens and represented nearly every insect family. During Rippon's lifetime, it was one of the largest collections in private hands.

In 1910, facing advancing age and diminishing health, Rippon printed a circular detailing his collection and explaining that it was for sale. However, he died in 1917 with his collection unsold. Ten months later his widow wrote to the Museum's director, Dr W. Evans Hoyle, offering the collection for £1,000. The Rippon collection was eventually moved to the Museum in 1918. The Museum's Annual Report for 1917-18 called it the 'most important event in the Zoological Department'.

Above and right: ***Triodes minos*** **Cramer.**

Rossetti's *Fair Rosamund* becomes part of Wales's national art collection.

This striking oil painting was created by Dante Gabriel Rossetti in 1861, some twelve years after the London-born artist had founded the Pre-Raphaelite Brotherhood with John Everett Millais and William Holman Hunt. They believed that the Classical poses and compositions of Raphael had been a corrupting influence on art, and wanted to bring the vitality of earlier Italian painting to British art – hence the name Pre-Raphaelite.

Many early works by Rossetti (1828-1882) featured Elizabeth Siddal, whom he married in 1860. However, the model for this painting was Fanny Cornforth. She was a frequent Rossetti sitter who became his housekeeper and companion after Elizabeth's death in 1862, apparently from an overdose of opium tincture laudanum.

Fair Rosamund depicts the mistress of Henry II. She was a figure of romance who, according to legend, was killed by the king's wife, Queen Eleanor. The painting was displayed at Penarth's Turner House Gallery in the collection of wealthy local philanthropist James Pyke Thompson until, in 1921, the Gallery and its collections were transferred to the Museum.

Rossetti himself was an intriguing character, becoming a virtual recluse after his wife's death. He had been so overcome with grief at her funeral that he had placed the only copy of his complete works of poetry in the coffin with her. In 1870 he had her body exhumed to retrieve his verses, much of which were subsequently published. He won support from the great art and social critic John Ruskin, but criticism of his paintings caused him to withdraw from public exhibitions and to concentrate on private commission work.

Right: *Fair Rosamund* (1861) by Dante Gabriel Rossetti.

TURNER HOUSE
GALLERY

Wealthy corn merchant James Pyke Thompson opens a people's gallery.

Penarth's James Pyke Thompson conceived the idea of a gallery offering art for all in 1888. He wanted to advance one of his social ambitions: that the public could view museum and gallery exhibits on a Sunday, the day that afforded most people the time to view. Turner House therefore became known as The Sunday Gallery.

Left: The front of Turner House Gallery.

Turner House was designed by Edwin Seward, one of the most artistic young architects of his time. It was built on James Pyke Thompson's own land, by the gates of his house in Penarth.

The structure was intended to be attractive in appearance but modest in character. Its central feature was a red brick arch featuring a balcony and balustrade. Exterior walls were decorated with large panels of sgraffito, a technique in which marks are scratched into a glaze to reveal differently coloured clay beneath. At the time, the style was undergoing a revival in popularity in Britain.

The cost of the building was reported to be about £5,000. Its name had been suggested by English art critic Sir Frederick Wedmore in tribute to JMW Turner who had died in 1851. Sir Frederick helped Pyke Thompson bring together a collection that included works by Turner and Pre-Raphaelite painter Dante Gabriel Rossetti. There were also examples of porcelain. The gallery was housed on the first floor, with the downstairs used as accommodation for the custodian.

Turner House had three launch ceremonies – an informal opening, a garden party and a formal event. There were around 200 guests at the informal gathering. They had been invited by Pyke Thompson and his wife Anne, and represented the leading intellectual, commercial and social circles of Cardiff and Penarth. During the first Sunday opening, on 1 July, 1888, between 350 and 400 people of all classes visited.

Pyke Thompson continued to make acquisitions to his collection until he died in 1897. However, without his support and enthusiasm the gallery gradually lost the public's interest. Attendance figures dwindled. In 1921, the trustees handed over Turner House Gallery and its contents to the National Museum of Wales.

During the Second World War, the house was used by the RAF Women's Section. As hostilities neared an end it was decided that Turner House would show temporary exhibitions and works from the National Museum's reserve collection. With some slight structural modification, the gallery re-opened in 1950.

Dozens of items of art are bequeathed to the Welsh public by a prosperous benefactor.

James Pyke Thompson (1846-1897) was committed to the artistic life of Cardiff and Penarth, but there was so much more to him than that. He was a Trustee of West Grove Unitarian Church, Cardiff, a Liberal politician and a county magistrate. He was a key figure at corn merchants Spiller & Co until 1892 when he retired.

Born in Bridgwater, Somerset, he was one of eight children. His family moved to Cardiff in 1857, and seven years later his father, Charles, became chairman of a well-known corn mill. At eighteen years old, James joined his father at the firm, then known as Spiller & Co. Soon, he replaced the grindstones with new steam-powered rollers. By 1881, with Cardiff one of Britain's biggest grain importers, he was a director of the firm. He lived at Redlands, Plymouth Road, Penarth. The house was in the centre of the town, in extensive grounds with splendid views of the Bristol Channel.

Pyke Thompson used part of his wealth to assemble a collection of fine art, mainly nineteenth-century watercolours. In 1888 he placed part of his collection on public display at the Turner House Gallery, next to his home. He continued to collect and display art, including JMW Turner's *Transept of Ewenny Priory, Glamorganshire* and his prized *Fair Rosamund* by Rossetti. In 1895 he was elected chairman of the Municipal Museum Fine Arts Sub-Committee.

He lent a substantial part of his collection for display at the Museum and drew up a report on the future development of the Museum's fine art collection. He advocated that 'local artists and Welsh artists, whether living or dead, should be represented more or less fully according to their position in the world of art. Beyond this our choice should be limited to the very finest painters of the day.'

During his lifetime, Pyke Thompson donated £3,000 to Cardiff Museum and its successor, the National Museum of Wales. A further £3,000 was given to encourage the Museum to open on Sundays. This money was used to help secure the four-acre site for the new premises at Cathays Park. The Museum later named a gallery in the new building after him.

In 1898, 149 watercolours, a small number of oil paintings, a portfolio of etchings and three cases of British and continental porcelain from his collection were bequeathed to the Museum. The whole of Pyke Thompson's collection was reunited when the trustees of Turner House Gallery presented the building and its contents to the National Museum of Wales in 1921.

Above: James Pyke Thompson.
Right: *The Palace of Biebrich* (1817) by JMW Turner.

A ground-breaking collection of fossils is donated to the Museum.

David Davies, a south Wales plant fossil collector, was a pioneer in his field. The Museum was offered his remarkable collection in the 1920s.

Above: David Davies.
Top and right: A fossilized fern, one of over 16,000 fossils in the collection.

Although born in humble circumstances, David Davies (1871-1931) obtained academic certificates in mining, geology, machine drawing, mathematics and electricity.

At twenty-one he obtained a first-class certificate as colliery manager and went on to get a first-class diploma in electrical engineering. At the same time he started to collect fossils, and soon earned the nickname 'Dafydd Ffossil'.

In 1896 Davies settled in Clydach Vale where he spent much time studying and identifying fossils. He noted that different coal seams were associated with different types of plant fossil, and he used this information to interpret changes in the vegetation that produced the coals.

In 1908, he was invited to talk on the subject to the National Association of Colliery Managers. His reputation grew and, in 1920, Davies led a field trip for the Geologists' Association, and lectured to the Manchester Geological and Mining Society, the British Association for the Advancement of Science in Cardiff and the Geological Society of London. In 1921, he was awarded an honorary MSc from University College Cardiff.

However, his collection's growth presented storage problems, and in 1922 he offered it to the Museum. He stipulated that his specimens be kept safe, clearly labelled and accessible for further study. He requested that small representative collections were made available to the colleges of the University of Wales. His donation included field notebooks, catalogues and manuscripts.

Davies continued to send his work to the Museum. In 1926 he was elected to the Museum's council and science committee. After his death, 15 tons of unbroken shale were moved to the Museum. Davies's research was pioneering, and the result is a unique reference collection of plant fossils, containing 16,000 specimens.

Fact and fiction collide as archaeologist and newspaper men tell a great story to help us understand the past.

Caerleon is one of the most important Roman military sites in Europe. So when money was needed to excavate the amphitheatre in the 1920s, the Museum's director, distinguished archaeologist Sir Mortimer Wheeler (1890-1976), enlisted the help of the *Daily Mail* … and some handy myths.

In AD 74 or 75, with the final conquest of the tribal areas of south Wales underway, the Romans built a legionary fortress at Caerleon. It was named Isca, after the nearby River Usk.

Since the twelfth century, the Roman amphitheatre at Caerleon had been regularly misidentified as the site of King Arthur's Round Table. In 1190, *Giraldus Cambrensis* (Gerald of Wales) wrote: 'It was here that the Roman legates came to seek audience at the great Arthur's famous court'.

Gerald had been heavily influenced by Geoffrey of Monmouth's fictional epic, *History of the Kings of Britain,* which located Arthur's court at Caerleon, but was later described as 'the fruits of a lively historical imagination'. Nevertheless, popular Welsh and French romances perpetuated this folklore – and all this encouraged the *Daily Mail* in 1926 to treble their first offer for exclusive rights and daily reports on the excavation of the site.

Sir Mortimer was accused of shameless exploitation, but his strategy produced the vital funds, and the amphitheatre was excavated and preserved as a national monument. When he took the post of Keeper of the London Museum in 1926, his wife Tessa assumed direction of the excavation but he continued to mastermind the work from afar, all the while supplying the *Daily Mail* with sensational stories about their discoveries.

Left: Tessa Wheeler at the excavation site.
Above: Sir Mortimer Wheeler.

The National Museum of Wales welcomes a king and queen.

King George V visited Cardiff in 1927 to finish the job he had started in 1912.

Greeted by vast crowds, King George V and Queen Mary arrived in an open landau to open the National Museum of Wales in Cardiff on 21 April 1927. The Museum had been founded in 1907 under the Royal Charter of Incorporation granted by his father, and the King had laid the foundation stone in 1912, but construction was delayed by the First World War.

On arrival at the Museum, the King was given a ceremonial mallet, which he used to knock on the massive doors to gain admittance. Once inside, His Majesty praised the ideals of the founders of the Museum, as expressed by Lord Pontypridd in his Loyal Address in 1912 – 'to teach the world about Wales, and the Welsh people about their own Fatherland', referring to 'a shrine ... of Welsh antiquities'.

The ceremony included the Loyal Address of the Court of Governors and the Council by the Museum President Colonel the Lord Kenyon, the King's response and a religious service conducted by the Archbishop of Wales and the Archdruid of Wales. The BBC broadcast the programme of music, arranged by Sir Walford Davies, and the entire ceremony. The Lord Mayor of Cardiff arranged for amplifiers to be placed on 'almost every other tree' in Cathays Park in order to carry 'every word of the proceedings to the crowds'.

The King unveiled tablets naming three galleries after three of the Museum's major benefactors: James Pyke Thompson, creator of the Turner House Gallery, and shipping magnates William James Tatem (First Baron Glanely of St Fagans) and Sir William Reardon Smith.

Copies of the Loyal Address were specially printed and bound by the Gregynog Press.

Above and left: The Royal opening of the Museum in April 1927.

CYMRU

Tenuirostris?

Communis & Platyodon

My dear Sir

I entirely agree with you as far as I. Communis & I. Platyodon are concerned; the Oxford specimen belongs to the former my first views were clearly formed from a species which is either I. Tenuirostris or at least approaches more nearly to it than to ~~any other spe~~ either of the others in the form of its teeth – Little beauty (the name I give to your exquisite small specimen belongs to it – also the ~~single head~~ fragment of a head which I have of yours – marked but clearly in haste & incorrectly I. communis I suppose before you fully made out your species – Miss Congreves head which was sent to me was probably of the same species but I neglected to examine the teeth – I wish you would do so – which as it is now again in her possession you may easily do – – ~~I have~~ In these species my views were perfectly correct – I have drawn both – from specimens now before me & wish you to examine your specimens

1927 - 1937

The papers of an influential geologist are donated to the Museum

The H. T. De la Beche Collection is a major part of the archives in the Museum's Department of Geology. It contains 2,000 items of correspondence including examples from Prince Albert and Charles Darwin, journals of his travels and personal items such as photographs. Official correspondence concerning the Geological Survey forms almost half the collection and provides a fascinating insight into the day-to-day scientific endeavours of the first half of the nineteenth century.

Left: A page from one of De la Beche's notebooks. Above: Henry Thomas De la Beche.

Henry Thomas De la Beche (1796-1855) was born in London, but his family's wealth came from sugar plantations in Jamaica. He moved with his mother to Lyme Regis, Dorset, where an interest in geology was probably triggered by his acquaintance with geological pioneer and local fossil collector Mary Anning. Private means allowed him, like some contemporaries, to pursue geology as a gentlemanly pastime. In 1817 he joined the Geological Society of London, and the standing it afforded him provided the professional platform on which his subsequent career was built.

While mapping the rocks of Devon, De la Beche found himself in financial difficulty. Income from his Jamaican estate had fallen due to the abolition of the slave trade and a depression in the sugar trade. In 1832, he applied to the Government for funding to complete his Devon work and was granted £300.

In 1835, he was allowed to extend his work to the west, and the Geological Survey of Cornwall was formed. From this grew the Geological Survey of Great Britain – today's British Geological Survey. In 1837, recognising the economic importance of the South Wales Coalfield, De la Beche moved his Geological Survey to Swansea.

De la Beche established the Museum of Economic Geology (later the Geological Museum and now part of the Natural History Museum, London), the Royal School of Mines and the Mining Record Office. In founding these organizations, De la Beche pioneered the idea of publicly funded science.

The geologist's papers were donated to the Museum in the 1930s. The collection was put together by Frederick J. North (1889-1968), the Museum's first keeper of geology. North hoped to produce a biography of De la Beche. However, little information about him was available until the discovery of a box crammed with letters and manuscripts in the attic of De la Beche's great-grandson, Colonel John Illtyd Dillwyn Nicholl, of Merthyr Mawr.

A bold painting by an important Welshman is bought by the Museum.

Richard Wilson (c. 1713-1782) was one of the foremost British landscape painters of his time. His grand, brooding landscapes, all an exquisite study in light and shade, were to greatly inspire the works of Turner and Constable.

Above: Portrait of Richard Wilson by Anton Raphael Mengs.
Right: *Pembroke Town and Castle* (1774) by Richard Wilson.

Wilson was born in Penegoes, Montgomeryshire where his father was a Rector. His mother was related to several local wealthy landowners, and her brother was the very rich and powerful Sir George Wynne. It might well have been Sir George who recognised Wilson's talent early on. In 1730, he sent him to London to be apprenticed for six years with a leading painter of the time, Thomas Wright, and then later helped him to set set up his own studio.

In 1750 Wilson left London for Venice where the artist Francesco Zuccarelli encouraged him to concentrate on landscape views – a Venetian genre popular with British collectors. A year later he moved to Rome, where he obtained several commissions from English aristocrats and, in anticipation of their continued support, he returned to London in 1756.

In 1768 Wilson became a founding member of the Royal Academy of. At his peak, Wilson sold works to an increasing number of famous patrons, but his career faltered around 1770. As a result he soon took to drink. He was taken back to the family home in Wales where he died on 11 May 1782.

Pembroke Town and Castle was painted before 1767, when the picture was reproduced as an engraving. Wilson boldly exploits the sweep of the river and the patterns of the reflections of the castle and town. The picture was probably commissioned by William Vaughan of Cors-y-gedol, a major north Wales landowner and the first president of the Society of Cymmrodorion. The purchase of this painting in 1930, with the help of the Art Fund, was the foundation of the Museum's collection of this major Welsh artist's work.

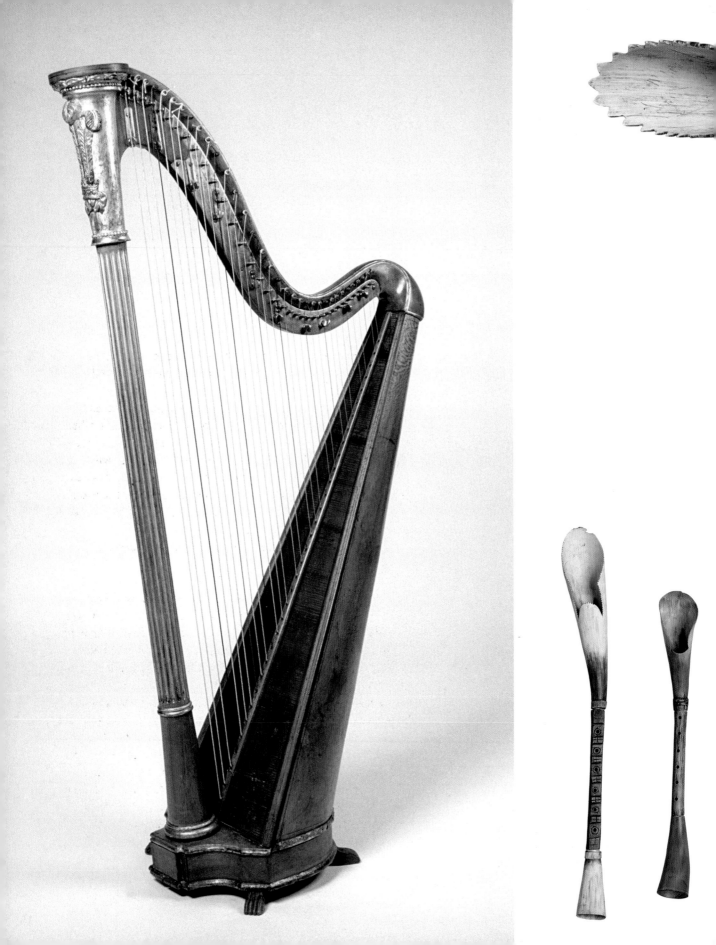

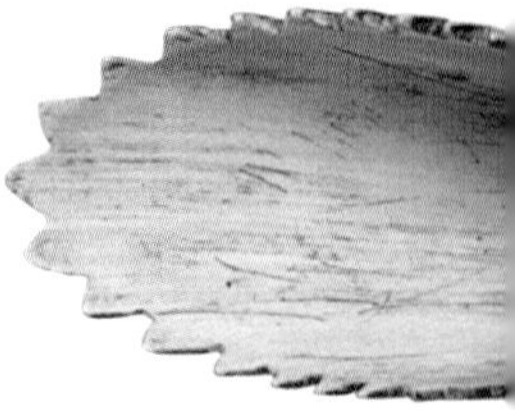

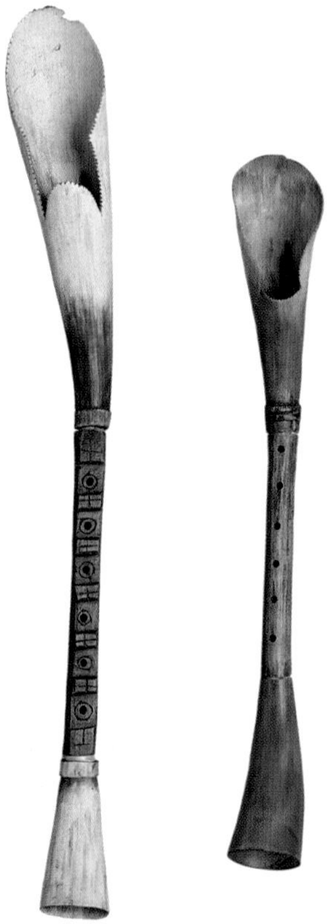

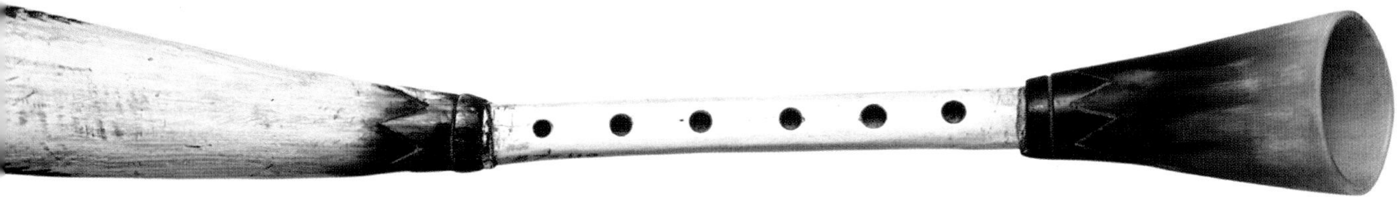

The music of Welsh life lives on.

The laws of Welsh ruler Hywel Dda (c. 940-50) specify that every master employing a *pencerdd* (chief musician) should give him the necessary harp, *crwth* and *pibgorn*. Today, these traditional Welsh instruments can be found at St Fagans.

Far left: The Museum's triple harp, which can now be seen in Oriel 1 in St Fagans. Above and left: Examples of the 'pibgorn' flute.

The Welsh *pibgorn*, or hornpipe, is one of the oldest Welsh instruments known. The Museum has three specimens from the eighteenth century, featuring an animal horn at either end, with the pipe itself of wood or bone.

It is essentially a single pipe with six finger holes and a thumb hole. There is a horn bell at one end to project the sound, and a horn wind-cap at the other to collect and funnel the wind through a reed. The *pibgorn* was used for passing the time on the cattle droves, possibly with dance music. We know that it was still being played by shepherds on Anglesey as late as 1870 and William Meredith Morris, writing in the early twentieth century, recalled a *pibgorn* being played in north Pembrokeshire as late as 1875.

The *crwth* was a forerunner of the violin, but was obsolete by 1800.

The triple harp – with three rows of strings – originated in Italy and appeared in Britain in the early seventeenth century. It was quickly adopted by Welsh harp players and became so popular that by the eighteenth century it was generally known as the Welsh harp.

Augusta Waddington Hall (1802-1896), better known as Lady Llanover, was a keen promoter of Welsh music and was particularly fond of the triple harp. She encouraged harpists and harp makers to live on her estate in Llanover, Gwent, and held many *eisteddfodau* in which the harp featured strongly. Bassett Jones of Cardiff, one of the most highly regarded makers of the period, made many fine triple harps for these events. They were frequently donated as prizes. The collections at St Fagans house several of his instruments. Until death, Lady Llanover remained a fervent champion of what she considered to be traditional Welsh culture.

After the early twentieth century triple harps became almost abandoned in Wales in favour of the modern pedal harp.

A museum that explores life in a far-flung outpost of the mighty Roman Empire.

Almost 2,000 years ago, the Romans dominated much of north Africa and the near East. Their settlements in Wales were near the edge of the then-known world. Approximately AD 75, a fortress was founded at Caerleon, one of only three permanent legionary bases in Roman Britain. Today, partly due to the efforts of an amateur antiquarian, we can explore the settlement at the National Roman Legion Museum.

It was only in the 1800s that the people of a new, industrialised Wales began to understand how life had been lived in Roman times. John Jenkins, the owner of Mynde House in the grounds of Caerleon Castle, made substantial alterations to his land. In the process, extensive Roman remains were uncovered, and he invited amateur antiquarian John Lee to study and record the discoveries.

Lee, along with local landowner Sir Digby Mackworth, contributed greatly to the formation of the Caerleon Antiquarian Association.

Lee worked systematically, making detailed observations on the discoveries. He created plans of the remains and etchings showing the objects and uncovered remains. This was fortunate, as it is the only record we have of the Roman bathing complex there – it seems that Jenkins later removed all trace of the remains during landscaping work.

Lee published his findings in a pamphlet, *Remains of the Roman Villa &c &c In the Castle Grounds, Caerleon.* This was sold to supplement funds raised by the Caerleon Antiquarian Association to build a Museum of Antiquities in 1850. In 1930, the museum became part of the National Museum of Wales.

The National Roman Legion Museum lies inside what remains of the fortress, including the most complete amphitheatre in Britain and the only remains of a Roman legionary barracks on view anywhere in Europe. It researches, preserves and displays half a million objects from the Roman fortresses of Caerleon (*Isca*), Usk (*Burrium*) and their environs. It is an internationally important collection, which provides evidence for life in two major Roman military bases as well as life in the civilian settlements that grew up around them.

Right: The exterior of the old Legionary Museum of Caerleon.

NATIONAL MUSEUM OF WALES
LEGIONARY MUSEUM OF CAERLEON
OPEN
ADMISSION

An important collection wings its way to Cardiff – it features more than 11,000 insects.

Bees, wasps and ants might have seemed insignificant to many in the early years of the last century – but one man in particular knew that they provided important evidence about how natural Wales was developing.

Above and right: Original specimens from the Hallett collection.

Howard Mountjoy Hallett was born in 1878 in Devon, but his family moved to Cardiff around 1882. He became one of the most important insect experts in Wales. Hallett's interests were wide and varied, and he published notes on several insect groups. His chief interest, however, was in bees, wasps and ants. His lists of species recorded at sites in Glamorgan are impressive and fairly exhaustive. Two of his favoured collecting sites were Sully and Porthcawl. At Sully, he recorded the only confirmed Welsh records for four types of bee. Also from Sully, he added one type of ant to the British list. At Porthcawl, he recorded the last Welsh records for one type of bee and the only Welsh record of one type of wasp. Hallett's efforts to record the bees, ants and wasps – together known as aculeates – of his area ensured that Glamorgan was among the best-studied counties in Britain at the time.

Hallett was elected a member of the Cardiff Naturalists' Society in 1900 and became president in 1915. The same year he was elected to the Council of the National Museum of Wales, a position he held until his death.

Hallett's association with the Museum extended over forty years and his influence on the entomological collections held there cannot be overstated. His donations numbered more than 11,000 specimens, presented to the Museum on 15 September 1931 and representing 414 of the 470 species then known to inhabit the British Isles.

On 10 September 1956, at the age of seventy-eight, Hallett presented the Museum with a manuscript that provided an unparalleled insight into the changes to Wales's bees, wasps and ants over half a century.

It was called *List of Hymenoptera Aculeata of Wales and Monmouthshire*. His association both with the Museum and the Naturalists' Society continued until his death on 15 May 1958 at the age of eighty.

Old Cogan
H.M.Hallett
Sully,
H.M.Hallett.
3251

1937 - 1947

One of Britain's finest nineteenth-century bronzes is given as a gift to the Museum.

English sculptor and goldsmith Sir Alfred Gilbert preferred his *Icarus* to any of his other works. The figure from Greek mythology is a frequent personification of the dangers of youthful ambition, and Gilbert regarded the work as a form of psychological self-portrait. Acquired by a leading Welsh sculptor, it now belongs to Wales.

Welshman Sir William Goscombe John (1860-1952) was a great supporter of the Museum and it was he who donated *Icarus* in 1938. A unique bronze, it was a stunning addition to the collections. Profoundly influenced by Donatello, its exceptional quality had established Gilbert as the most influential sculptor of his generation.

Icarus started life as a commission by Frederic Leighton, the leading Classical artist of the period. The choice of subject was left to Gilbert. It was exhibited at the Royal Academy in 1884, along with his remarkable *Study of a Head*, and was received with general applause.

In Greek mythology, Icarus was the son of the inventor Daedelus. Provided with wings of wax and feathers by his father, Icarus flew too near the sun and crashed to the earth when the wax melted.

Gilbert (1854-1934) was a central – if idiosyncratic – participant in the New Sculpture movement that invigorated sculpture in Britain at the end of the nineteenth century. He studied in Paris, Rome and Florence. There, the significance of the Renaissance made a lasting impression on him and his art. He also worked in the studio of Austrian-born sculptor Sir J. Edgar Boehm and enthusiastically experimented with metallurgical innovations.

Gilbert's first work of importance was the charming group *Mother and Child*, followed by *The Kiss of Victory* and *Perseus Arming*, produced directly under the influence of the Florentine masterpieces he had studied. His *Eros* in Piccadilly Circus is still one of London's best-loved monuments.

Right: *Icarus* (1884) by Sir Alfred Gilbert.

An admired Welsh artist hands his own influential works and collection to the nation.

The leading Welsh sculptor at the dawn of the twentieth century, Sir William Goscombe John (1860-1952) donated many of his finest pieces, as well as his own collection of works by his contemporaries, to the Museum.

Left: *Sir William Goscombe John* (1902) by George Roilos.

Born in Cardiff, John was an influential figure, destined to become a lifelong patron and friend to art and artists in Wales. By fourteen he had started his career as an artist. He took drawing classes at the Cardiff School of Art then joined his father to work on the building of Cardiff Castle for the Third Marquess of Bute. His first job was to carve quaint grotesques on the shutters of the small dining room.

In 1881, he left for London and added Goscombe to his name, taken from his mother's Gloucestershire family. He became a carver in the London studio of Thomas Nicholls and, in 1884, entered the Royal Academy Schools. He pursued a dual role as craftsman by day and artist by night until 1887 when he won the Landseer Scholarship, which enabled him to set up a studio.

In 1888 he submitted work for a Royal Academy exhibition. Critic Edmund Gosse singled out his *Portrait of a Lady* as 'modelled with an enchanting sweetness of touch'. The sitter was the Swiss woman Marthe Weiss, whom he soon married. In 1889, he won the prestigious RA Gold Medal.

Goscombe John visited the studio of Rodin, whose influence is apparent in the Welshman's figure *Morpheus*. Other works included a life-size *Boy at Play* and *The Elf* – which, along with *Joyance*, is displayed in the grounds of St Fagans: National History Museum. In 1909 he joined the ranks of the Royal Academicians and two years later was knighted for services to Wales and Welsh art.

He became a founding member of the Royal Society of British Sculptors, a patron of the Museum and an original member of the Museum's Council. He presented the national collections with many of his finest pieces, as well as his own collection of works by his contemporaries.

It was he who designed the founding Seal of the National Museum of Wales, as well as the implements used by George V at the ceremony for laying the Museum's foundation stone.

SPHÆRA

IOANNIS DE SACRO BOSCO, EMENDATA.

Eliæ Vineti Santonis scholia in eandem Sphæram; ab ipso auctore restituta.

Adiunximus huic libro compendium in Sphæram per Pierium Valerianum Bellunensem,

Et

PETRI NONII SALACIENSIS demonstrationem eorum, quæ in extremo capite de climatibus Sacroboscius scribit de inæquali climatum latitudine, eodem Vineto interprete.

IN ME MORS,

IN ME VITA.

PARISIIS,

Apud Hieronymum de Marnef, & viduam Gulielmi Cauellat, sub Pelicano, Monte Diui Hilarij.

A unique book collection of world importance is left to the people of Wales.

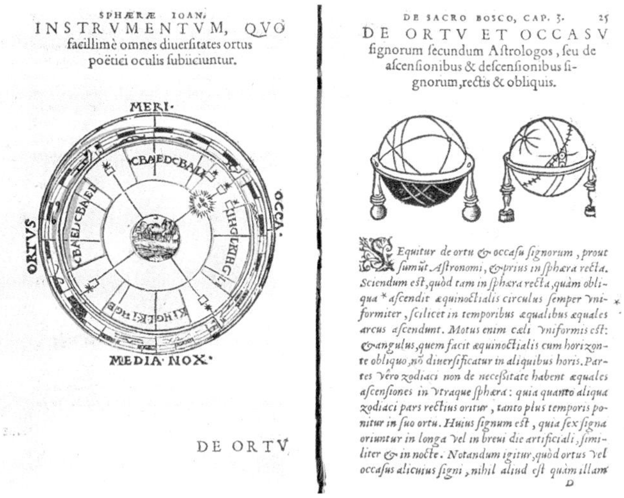

John Herbert James (1859-1939) was an incredible collector of books, who even built his own library to house his treasures. Since 1939 they have rested with the Museum.

The Boer War helped. In protest at Britain's involvement in the bloody dispute, James headed for Italy. While abroad he travelled widely and visited every port in the Mediterranean, collecting books wherever he went. These formed part of what would soon become a resource of major significance.

James was born at Brynteg, Merthyr Tydfil. He studied Latin at school in Merthyr and went on to Oxford to read classics, before reading law at Lincoln's Inn. In 1912 he built a library to house his extensive book collection at his home, The Cottage in Vaynor near Merthyr. This building of Bath stone, parquet floor and double windows sat on five arches with a tower projecting upwards – an echo of Italy among the Welsh hills.

On his death, James bequeathed his library collection, known as The Vaynor Collection, to the Museum. The collection consists of a number of valuable astronomical works from the sixteenth and seventeenth centuries. There are also remarkable first editions from Galileo and the second-century Greek astronomer Ptolemy.

The Vaynor Collection is housed in the Library in National Museum Cardiff. Besides general reference material, the Library holds a number of other important collections, such as special edition books from the Gregynog Press.

Approximately 3,000 volumes are added to the Library annually. At present, the collection consists of over 200,000 monographs and bound journals, and 1,200 periodicals are added every year.

Left: The title page of the 1577 edition of *Sphaera* by Johannes de Sacro Bosco, a mathematician who died about the middle of the thirteenth century.
Above: Pages from *Sphaera*.

A famous French kiss comes to Cardiff.

Auguste Rodin (1840-1917) was born into a working-class family in Paris. He was largely self-educated and began to draw aged ten. He applied to the École des Beaux Arts, the most prestigious art school in Paris, but was rejected three times. Instead, he attended Paris's School of Decorative Arts, and spent two decades working for several craftsmen.

Rodin entered the studio of French sculptor Albert Ernest Carrier-Belleuse as a chief assistant, where he worked until 1872. Three years later, he visited Italy, where he drew on the work of Donatello and Michelangelo, which had a profound effect on his artistic direction. By 1900, his artistic reputation was firmly established.

Instead of copying traditional academic postures, Rodin used amateur models, street performers and dancers. His models moved about and took natural positions. He made quick sketches in clay that were later refined then cast in bronze or carved in marble.

The Kiss (c. 1887) was originally intended for the monumental *The Gate of Hell*, commissioned in 1880 for a planned museum of art in Paris. However, it was removed early on as Rodin felt the joy of the couple was at odds with the writhing and tortured souls featured in *The Gate*.

Its blend of eroticism and idealism makes *The Kiss* one of art's great images of love. The couple are the adulterous lovers Paolo Malatesta and Francesca da Rimini, who were killed by Francesca's husband – and Paolo's brother – Giovanni. They appear in Dante's *Inferno*, which describes how the lovers' passion grew as they read the Arthurian legend of Lancelot and Guinevere together – the book can just be seen in Paolo's hand.

Purchased in Paris by Gwendoline Davies, one of the Davies sisters of Gregynog, in 1912, *The Kiss* was a prominent feature in the *Loans Exhibition* organized by the Museum in 1913 in Cardiff's City Hall. Gwendoline Davies donated it to the Museum in 1940.

Left: *The Kiss* by Auguste Rodin.

The great Welsh painter meets the great Welsh poet.

Augustus John (1878-1961) was a Welsh painter, draughtsman and etcher. He painted many distinguished contemporaries including Thomas Hardy, W. B. Yeats and George Bernard Shaw. Perhaps one of his most famous portraits is of his fellow countryman, Dylan Thomas.

Born in Tenby, Pembrokeshire, Augustus John went to the Slade School of Art – probably the most progressive art school in London – with his older sister Gwen. He won several prizes at the Slade and became well known even before his graduation.

His subject, Dylan Thomas (1914-1953,) is widely regarded as one of the twentieth century's most influential lyrical poets. His hallmark is his idiosyncratic and surreal introspection, and his startling imagery. Although Thomas was primarily a poet, he also published short stories and film scripts and performed his works live and in radio broadcasts. His most renowned work, *Under Milk Wood*, set in the fictional Welsh seaside village of Llareggub (spell it backwards..), was what Thomas called a 'play for voices' and expressed a remarkable poetic sensibility.

By 1934, Thomas moved to London as he hoped to achieve a literary reputation outside Wales. There he quickly secured publishing deals that brought him immediate acclaim. In 1935, John introduced Caitlin MacNamara, who had been his lover for several years, to Dylan Thomas at the Fitzroy Tavern. Thomas and Caitlin married in 1937.

This portrait is one of two versions by John. Both probably date from late 1937 or early 1938 when Thomas and his wife were staying at her mother's house in Hampshire not far from John's home at Fryern Court. The artist recalled: 'I got him to sit for me twice, the second portrait being the more successful: provided with a bottle of beer he sat very patiently.'

This portrait was given to the Museum by the Contemporary Art Society in 1942.

Above: Augustus John.
Right: *Dylan Thomas* (1937-8) by Augustus John.

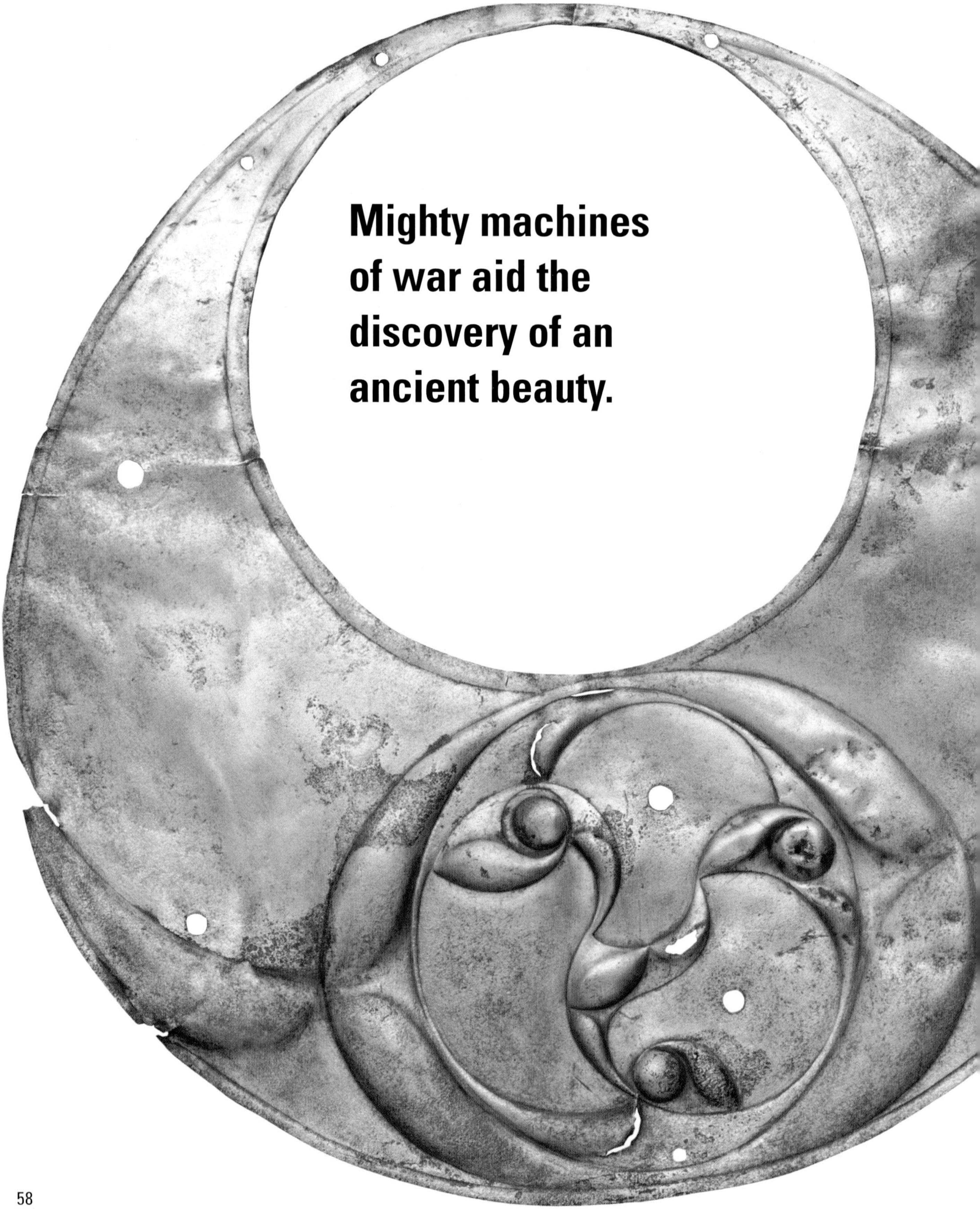

Mighty machines of war aid the discovery of an ancient beauty.

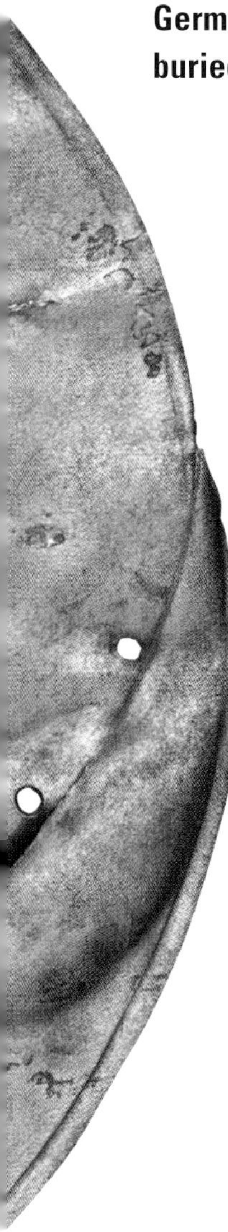

This bronze plaque is one of Britain's most celebrated Iron Age finds. But were it not for the planned arrival in Wales of bomb-laden aircraft designed to wreak destruction on Nazi Germany, it could still be buried in an Anglesey bog.

At the RAF base in Valley, Anglesey, runways had to be prepared for substantial extension. They would be used by B-17s and partner craft such as the B-24 Liberators from the USA and Canada.

An area was identified for the runways, and dredging of the area began. However, during construction work, one unfortunate lorry driver found his vehicle embedded in the soggy ground. A tractor arrived to assist in the recovery, using a large chain that had been found in the bog.

A curious engineer became interested in the three-metre chain, which had loops attached at equal distances along its length. He reported it, and other objects found at the site, to the Museum. On examination, the chain was identified as a gang-chain or slave-chain, and some 2,000 years old. The loops were for human necks.

RAF workmen dug out more remarkable Iron Age objects and, in 1943, Cyril Fox, Director of the National Museum of Wales and a leading archaeologist, was called in. Dredging was halted, and over 150 objects from pre-Roman times were discovered. They were taken to the Museum at Cardiff, to be documented and catalogued.

Among the items discovered were a number of decorated objects in the Early Celtic Art style, cauldrons, horse and chariot fittings, weapons, blacksmith's tools and bars of iron probably used for trading.

The items represent Early Celtic art at its finest. The plaque in particular has been pivotal to the understanding of British Celtic Art during the second and first centuries BC.

Thought to be votive offerings to the gods of the lake, they would have been thrown into the sacred lake of Llyn Cerrig Bach. Many of these objects must have belonged to individuals who enjoyed high rank within their communities. Some of the objects had apparently travelled far from their original place of use and creation, suggesting this was a religious site of some influence.

Radiocarbon dating of animal bones from the site and re-analysis of the bronze objects suggests that the offerings were thrown into Llyn Cerrig Bach on a number of occasions between 300 BC and AD 100.

Left: Ornamental bronze plaque with triskele detail.
Right: Bridle bit, discovered at Llyn Cerrig Bach.

Discover the largest treasure of St Fagans.

The past half-century has seen more than forty original buildings from many periods of Welsh history relocated to St Fagans – one of Europe's foremost open-air museums. They are watched over by a friend who has stood in the same place for more than 400 years. It remains a key part of the visitor's experience.

St Fagans Castle is a sixteenth-century manor house that was donated to the people of Wales by the Earl of Plymouth in 1946. It's a piece of history, lovingly restored to its late nineteenth-century style and set in beautiful historic gardens.

Sir Edward Lewis of Van bought St Fagans Castle and its grounds in 1616 from Sir William Herbert. The new owner immediately set about improving the building and it became the chief residence of the Lewis family. In 1730 the Earl of Plymouth married the heiress Elizabeth Lewis and took ownership of the castle. During the 1760s some decoration work was carried out but by 1815 the building had become sadly neglected.

The Castle was restored in the 1850s and was eventually generously given by the Third Earl of Plymouth to the Museum.

A Grade 1 listed building, the Castle is an excellent example of Elizabethan architecture. Today, the interiors are furnished to reflect the lives of the family in residence at the end of the nineteenth century. The Castle boasts rich tapestries, opulent rosewood and oak furniture and beautiful family paintings.

The formal gardens surrounding the Castle were once the sanctuary of the Earl of Plymouth and his family, who used the house as their summer home. The gardens include the exquisite Rosery, the Italian Garden and the elegant parterre and castle terraces, which overlook the medieval fishponds.

The Museum opened on 1 July 1948 in the Castle grounds. Today, it is Wales's most popular visitor attraction.

Above: A fountain in the Castle gardens.
Above: St Fagans Castle
Right: The Castle's Coed Coch Library.

Above: The Third Earl of Plymouth (front) with his family, outside St Fagans Castle.
Right: The Plymouth family.

A true patron.

On 4 February 1946, the Third Earl of Plymouth, with his mother the Countess of Plymouth, called on Sir Cyril Fox, then director of the Museum. They offered St Fagans Castle, its gardens and eighteen acres of land as the basis of an open-air museum. It was a big step forward for the Museum.

The castle and grounds at St Fagans, near Cardiff, had been part of the Plymouth family's estate since 1730. By the start of the twentieth century, the Earldom of Plymouth also held properties in Flintshire, Worcestershire and Shropshire.

The family has always supported Amgueddfa Cymru – National Museum Wales: The Second Earl of Plymouth, Ivor Miles Windsor-Clive (1889-1943) was Treasurer from 1929 to 1933 and President from 1933 to 1937. The Third Earl of Plymouth, Other Robert Ivor Windsor-Clive (born 1923), was President from 1967 to 1972.

In order to develop the idea of an open-air facility fully, the Museum felt it was necessary to acquire additional land. The Earl readily agreed to the purchase 'at a nominal sum' of around eighty acres of enclosed parkland next to the Castle grounds.

He went on to become the founder member of the Museum's Patrons Scheme. Over ten years, the Scheme has grown to more than 125 committed and enthusiastic members who provide invaluable support.

The Earl's family seat is Oakly Park, near Ludlow, Shropshire.

A chance to take a lesson in the colourful international education of a young eighteenth-century aristocrat.

Like many well-to-do young men of his time, Sir Watkin Williams-Wynn (1749-1789) took the European Grand Tour to supplement his more traditional education. This 'gap year' brought him into contact with some wonderful high culture – and around 180 years later the people of Wales were to benefit from this.

Above and right: *Sir Watkin Williams Wynn, 4th Bt, Thomas Apperley and Captain Edward Hamilton* (1768-72) by Pompeo Batoni.

June 1768 must have been a thrilling time for Sir Watkin Williams-Wynn. In his late teens, this fabulously rich young owner of the Wynnstay estate near Wrexham was about to set off on his nine-month journey around France, Switzerland and Italy. He planned to enjoy theatre, opera, sightseeing and lessons in music and dance. He would move in high society, and collect and commission art.

He set out with Thomas Apperley of Plas Grono, near Wrexham, who had been with him at Oxford and Edward Hamilton, a cavalry officer and amateur musician. After visiting Paris and Florence they arrived in Rome in November, where Sir Watkin commissioned this portrait from Pompeo Batoni (1708–1787), the most celebrated painter in the city.

Batoni was highly influential, his style incorporating elements of French Rococo, Bolognese classicism and nascent Neoclassicism. He is now well known as a painter of elegant and dignified portraits, his best works displaying exquisite colour and brushwork, and vivid characterization. His work was particularly appreciated by British gentry, and many Grand Tour travellers visited his studio.

In this painting, Sir Watkin stands on the left holding a crayon and a copy of a Raphael fresco. At the table, Apperley draws his patron's attention to a passage from Dante's *Divine Comedy*. Hamilton, a flute in his hand, gestures admiringly to Apperley's display of erudition. An allegorical statue of Painting in a niche behind them emphasizes the men's love of the arts.

This is the largest of Batoni's Grand Tour portraits. During Sir Watkin's lifetime, it hung at his London residence, Wynn House, in St James Square. The painting was bought by the Museum in 1947 for £230.

1947-1957

A pioneering open-air folk museum opens.

St Fagans: National History Museum is Wales's most popular heritage attraction. More than forty original buildings from different historical periods have been painstakingly re-erected in the 100-acre parkland of the magnificent St Fagans Castle, near Cardiff. Previously known as the Welsh Folk Museum and the Museum of Welsh Life, it opened in 1948. It is now one of Europe's foremost open-air museums.

A practical interest in bygones developed at the Cardiff Museum around the turn of the twentieth century. In 1926, such collections were placed on permanent display in the Welsh Bygones Gallery at the new National Museum of Wales. This made the Museum the UK's first national institution to create a scientifically ordered collection illustrating folk culture and related industries.

Enthusiasm grew further after the Museum's Director, Sir Cyril Fox, visited Sweden in 1930 and saw examples of open-air folk museums. Three years later, a sub-department of folk culture and industries was formed within the Department of Archaeology. It was the first of its kind in Britain; its purpose 'to provide the people of Wales with a source of hitherto untapped self knowledge.'

The unexpected gift of St Fagans Castle by the Third Earl of Plymouth in 1946 presented the perfect opportunity to bring these ideals to fruition. The Welsh Folk Museum was modelled on Skansen, the museum of vernacular Swedish architecture in Stockholm. The new attraction at St Fagans had an influential advocate in Iorwerth Peate, a member of museum staff since 1926 and widely known as a poet and scholar. He became the first head of the folk museum.

St Fagans now illustrates and interprets the daily life and work of the people of Wales from Celtic times to the present day. Apart from the re-erected buildings, St Fagans also houses a sound archive and exhibitions of costumes, traditional crafts, domestic and farming implements and vehicles. There is a small working farm with local native livestock breeds, and craftspeople exhibit traditional skills.

In spring 2007, a new gallery, Oriel 1, was opened specifically to explore issues of contemporary Welsh identities, bringing the story of the people of Wales bang up to date.

Above: Iorwerth Peate, the first head of the innovative new open-air museum.
Right: The plaque commemorating the opening of the Welsh Folk Museum – now St Fagans: National History Museum.

JE·ME·FIE·EN·DIEU
1947

Above: Staff preparing items for loan in the 1950s.
Right (top): School pupils in the 1970s handling objects on loan from the Museum.
Right (bottom): The Outreach Service on the road today.

The 'Travelling Museum' is pioneered.

Among the most significant achievements of the Museum since its inception was the creation in 1948 of the innovative Schools Service, one of the first such large-scale ventures in the UK.

The Museum had worked with schools from the early 1920s, but the idea of an extended, more systematic national scheme was not conceived until the 1940s. Inaugurated in 1948, the Schools Service was run jointly by the Museum, which provided the accommodation, and the Welsh Joint Education Committee, which provided the funds. It was the most ambitious service of its kind in the UK, and came to be envied and copied by other museums.

The aim of the service was to interest, inspire and teach through objects. As well as assisting schools, the service added something extra and new, with its emphasis on loaning out objects or specimens, particularly those that could be handled. Most included in the scheme were originals but some were high quality replicas or models. The service covered all areas of the Museum's collections. However, the art collection was particularly welcomed by schools at a time when access to art reproductions was difficult and access to original works was rare.

During the 1990s, the collection came to be used by the wider community, including university students and student teachers, local history organizations and older people's groups, television companies, theatres, art centres, environmental groups, special needs centres and home learners. In 2000, it was renamed the Outreach Service to better reflect the way it is now used and enjoys ongoing support from the Friends of the Museum. In the past, access to the collection has always been behind the scenes. In the year of its centenary, the Museum is creating a 'shop window' for the treasures that travel in the Main Hall at National Museum Cardiff.

Wonderful works by Cézanne, Monet, Renoir, Van Gogh, Rodin and Turner are added to Wales's national art collection.

Gwendoline Davies (1882-1951) wrote that, like her sister Margaret, she derived 'great joy' from collecting art.

Gwendoline and Margaret were renowned for their love of art. Gwendoline's collection was bequeathed to the Museum in 1951, and still contains some of the Museum's most important works.

Gwendoline's collection was assembled between 1908 and 1924. Visits to Paris saw her acquire Monet's *San Giorgio Maggiore* and three of his famous *Waterlilies* paintings. She also bought Cézanne's *Midday, L'Estaque*. When on exhibition at the Burlington Fine Arts Club, it was remarked that this was 'one of the greatest of all Cézanne landscapes'.

Her bequest also included Renoir's *La Parisienne* – known affectionately by Museum visitors and staff alike as 'the Blue Lady'. It was one of only six oil paintings Renoir displayed at the *First Impressionist Exhibition* in 1874. Another great painting in Gwendoline's bequest is Van Gogh's *Rain: Auvers*. This landscape was painted in July 1890 and is one of the last pictures Van Gogh painted before he shot himself later the same month.

Sculptures in Gwendoline's collection include Rodin's famous *The Kiss*. She also collected works on paper, including Turner's *Rye, Sussex*, although her favourite artist seems to have been Welshman Augustus John – she collected more works by him than by any other artist.

Above: *Midday, L'Estaque* (1878-80) by Paul Cézanne
Right: *La Parisienne* (1874) by Pierre-Auguste Renoir.

A. Renoir. 74.

A solicitor's passion for pottery and porcelain leads to a huge collection – and a huge book.

The monumental tome *The Pottery and Porcelain of Swansea and Nantgarw* was published by Ernest Morton Nance in 1942. It remains the definitive work on the Welsh ceramics industry. A decade later, his impressive collection of ceramics was handed to Wales.

Swansea's Cambrian Pottery started life in the 1760s and closed in 1870. At that time, Ernest Morton Nance was only a toddler, having been born in Cardiff in 1868. By 1895, he was teaching Classics at Swansea Grammar School, and was becoming interested in Welsh pottery and porcelain. He began collecting the products of the country's ceramics industry, concentrating mainly on Cambrian wares.

Morton Nance went on to spend much of his career practising as a solicitor in London. He retired to live in St Ives, Cornwall, but his enthusiasm for Welsh ceramics continued undiminished. Following retirement, he collated his life's study into his book. In it he writes: 'At Swansea I was shown with pride specimens of local production and expressed the wish to possess some. I was told it would be impossible to find more than a few scattered pieces, because it was so scarce and so tightly held. Here was a challenge. A poor reason for forming a collection it is true – still, one which seemed adequate to me at the time.'

Morton Nance died in 1952 and his collection was bequeathed to the Museum. It featured around 1,500 pieces, doubling the Museum's collection of Welsh porcelain and trebling the items of Welsh pottery. It is a stunning overview of the history and the production methods of Welsh factories.

The collection contains many fine items of Swansea porcelain and noteworthy items of early nineteenth-century pottery from the Cambrian factory as well as numerous examples of the later transfer-printed wares. There are pieces from Swansea's Glamorgan Pottery and many from the short-lived period of porcelain manufacture at Nantgarw, near Caerphilly. The collection features a selection from Llanelli's South Wales Pottery that began production in 1840 and closed in 1922, marking the end of large-scale ceramic manufacture in Wales.

Left: A piece from Swansea's Cambrian Pottery.
Above: Ernest Morton Nance.

A uniquely Welsh set of love tokens arrives at St Fagans.

The custom of making small domestic and personal objects decorated with symbols of love, initials, names and dates was once common in rural communities. The carved lovespoon was almost exclusively a Welsh custom. A collection of lovespoons was therefore warmly welcomed by the Museum in the early 1950s.

Alan Whitehead of Abergavenny was a well-known twentieth-century collector of Welsh lovespoons. His collection was mostly obtained locally through dealers, and it was loaned to St Fagans in 1953. About half of the twelve spoons had once been part of another collection, that of Owen Evan Thomas. Whether they had been bought directly from Thomas or through dealers has been impossible to ascertain.

Carved wooden lovespoons were made throughout Wales from the middle of the seventeenth century until their decline towards the end of the nineteenth century – although they have recently seen a revival. They originally functioned essentially as a message from a young man to a young woman.

The time spent in decorating even a basic spoon was considerable. Every effort was made to carve the items from a single piece of wood, with no breaks or joins. The carving of initials was much more common than names, but the names that are to be found are invariably the girl's name. However, one spoon in the St Fagans collection has the name 'John' pierced through the handle. Did the recipient have so many suitors, that this one felt it necessary to identify himself?

Lovespoons began to become collectable at the beginning of the twentieth century, with Thomas and Ernest Pinto becoming the best-known collectors. Thomas obtained most of his collection at auctions in and around south Wales. By the late 1920s, he had built up a collection of some 1,200 wooden love tokens, including fifty lovespoons. He failed to sell his collection intact for £10,000 in the mid-1920s, so set about breaking it up and selling at auctions during the 1930s. Most of the Thomas collection was sold as individual pieces, and most have not been seen since.

Above and right: Lovespoons from the Museum's collection at St Fagans.

The great shell collectors.

The Melvill-Tomlin collection when bequeathed to the Museum was the second-largest shell collection in private hands containing 30,000 species and nearly one million specimens.

When James Cosmo Melvill (1845-1929) was eight years old he was given a small shell collection by his aunt, Mrs Hester Fenwick, starting a lifetime passion for him. Melvill built his collection by purchase and correspondence with many of the world's conchologists, collectors and dealers.

By 1900 Melvill had acquired a collection of 22,500 species which, at that time, was about half the world's known species. He described over a thousand new species of molluscs, from the Antarctic to the Arctic, Brazil, Australia and the Indo-Pacific Islands – including one species that he named after the aunt who had originally started his passion.

Melvill became acquainted with John Read le Brockton Tomlin (1864-1954), an equally enthusiastic collector. Like Melvill, Tomlin became interested in molluscs as a youth, collecting all over Britain and Europe. In 1902 he came into money, allowing him to give up teaching to devote himself to the study of molluscs.

Tomlin was one of a few collectors who continued to collect after the First World War. His knowledge of zoological nomenclature (the code for naming species) and his position as an associate member of the British Museum's molluscan section meant that his opinion was much sought, and was sometimes exchanged for specimens.

After Tomlin's death in 1954, the collection came to the Museum, along with his library of over 2,200 bound volumes, 7,000 pamphlets and an archive of over 700 letters from malacologists.

Tomlin was one the last of the great shell collectors, living through the period of change in the way molluscs were studied as animals rather than shells.

It has taken the Museum over 22 years to catalogue this historically important collection as a significant worldwide reference. There are very few places in the world where such a fine library and collection can be found together.

Above: (left) James Cosmo Melvill and (right) John Read le Brockton Tomlin.
Right: Shells and correspondence from the Melvill-Tomlin collection.

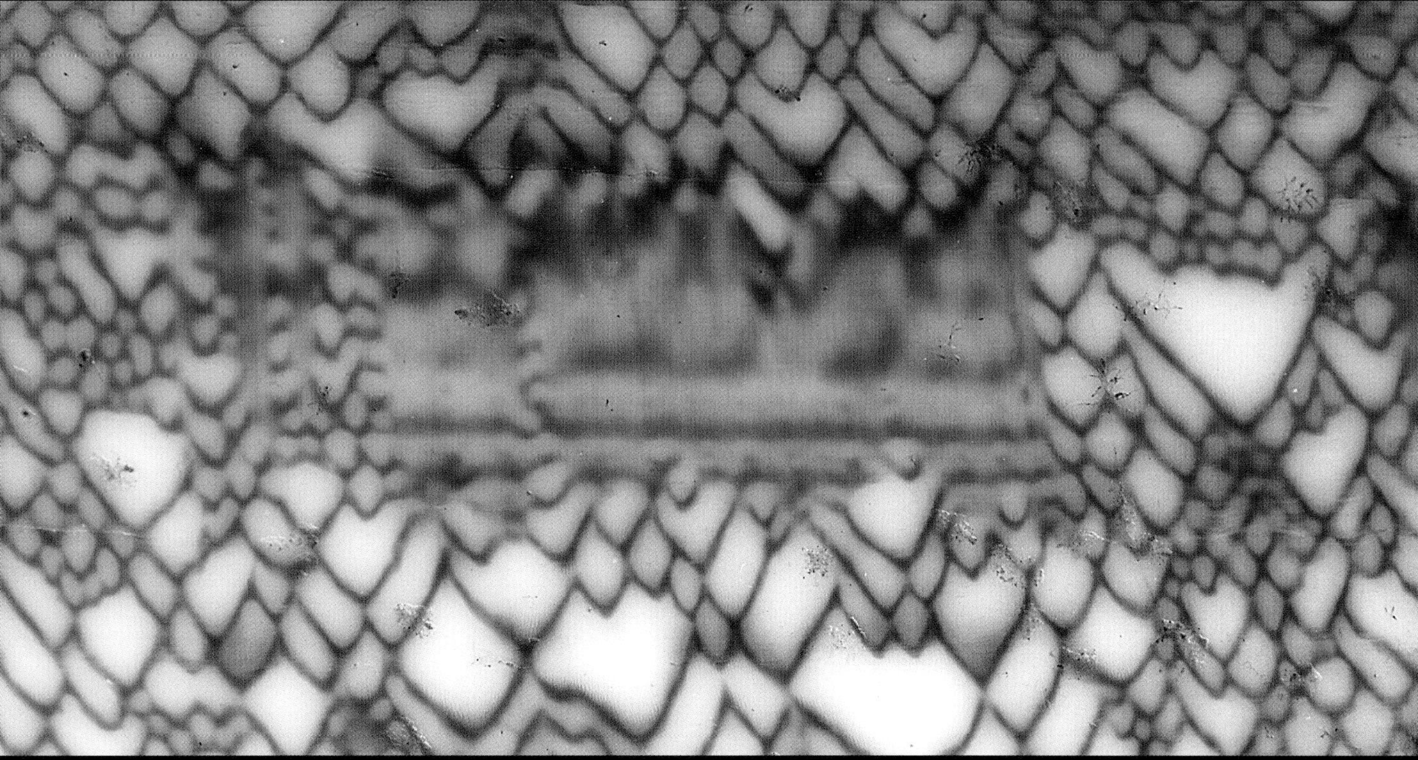

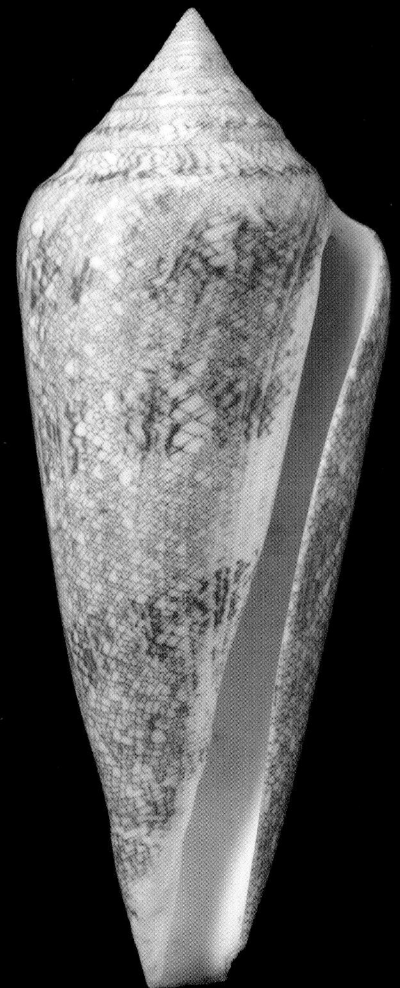

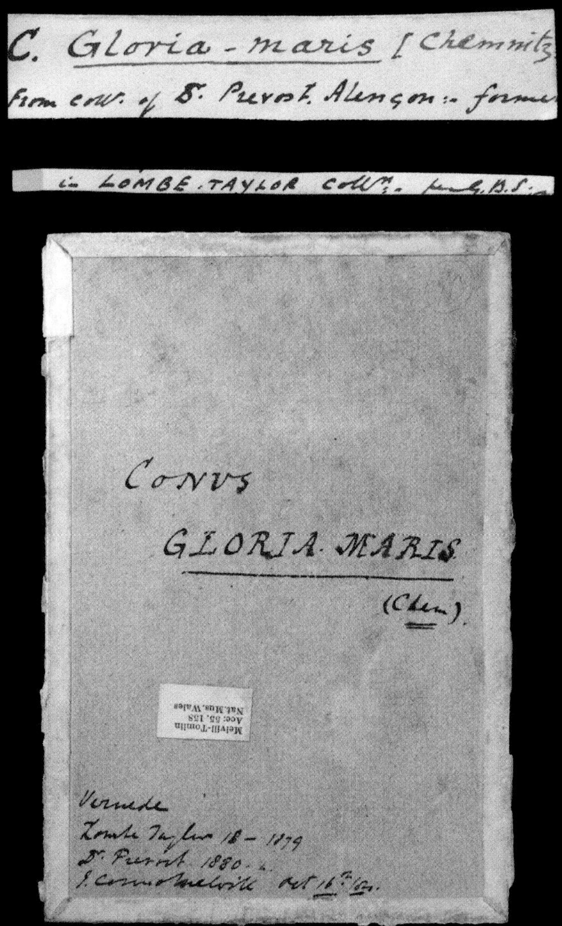
C. Gloria-maris [Chemnitz
from coll. of Dr. Prevost. Alençon :- former
in LOMBE.TAYLOR colln.
CONUS
GLORIA.MARIS
(Chem).
Melvill-Tomlin
Acc: 55. 158
Nat. Mus. Wales
Vernede
Dr. Prevost 1880.

The shock of the old.

Thomas Jones (1742-1803) was considered an unremarkable landscape painter, until fifty of his pictures came to auction at Christie's in 1954. The collection had been unknown, but it caused a sensation – the works were clearly so ahead of their time.

Thomas Jones was born at Trefonnen in Radnorshire. His parents planned for him to take Holy Orders, and he was educated at Jesus College, Oxford. However, he left in 1761 and turned to painting. He went to London and trained at William Shipley's Drawing School and then with the renowned Welsh painter Richard Wilson.

Wilson gave Jones a thorough grounding in his highly accomplished landscape style. Jones spent the next four years as a moderately successful painter.

In 1776, he went to Italy. He was ambitious and dreamed of emulating Wilson's fame. Although initially successful, he didn't manage to secure the patronage or alliances he had hoped for. He gradually gave up on advancing his professional status as a painter. However, he and his housekeeper – and lover – Maria Moncke left Rome and found cheap lodgings near the harbour in Naples, where he made open-air sketches for his own pleasure from the roof terrace. From this vantage point he produced a series of highly finished oil studies of the humble neighbouring buildings. These small paintings have a remarkable freshness and immediacy. Almost still life, they are bold, timeless and completely original.

However, when Jones returned to London in 1783, and exhibited his Italian views regularly at the Royal Academy, he struggled to find continued employment as an artist. In 1789, after his brother's death, he returned to Wales to run the family's estate, where he continued to paint and draw and to write his memoirs.

Upon the discovery of his Italian studies in the mid-fifties, his artistic reputation was transformed. Few artists have enjoyed such a dramatic reappraisal, so long after death.

Right: *Buildings in Naples* (1782) by Thomas Jones.

A sixteenth-century painting brings the powerful story of a strong-willed woman to Wales's museum visitors.

Katheryn of Berain (1534-1591) was married four times, each husband being a man of great influence. Her six children went on to found several dynasties of the Welsh gentry. She had at least sixteen stepchildren, thirty-two surviving blood grandchildren and innumerable descendants. Little wonder that she earned the nickname 'the Mother of Wales'.

A life that began colourfully for Katheryn of Berain, as King Henry VII's illegitimate great-granddaughter, proceeded to gain in interest. Much hinged on the fact that the preservation of inheritance in an Elizabethan family depended entirely on the institution of marriage and the direct heirs it produced. A family's reputation was maintained by engineering the most profitable marriages, which were essentially a business contract.

Katheryn's first husband was Sir John Salusbury. On the way to his funeral, it is said that she received an offer of marriage from Sir Richard Clough, a wealthy merchant from Denbigh. They married in 1567, and moved to Antwerp. Clough died in 1570 and Katheryn returned to Wales. By 1573 she was married to Maurice Wynn of Gwydir. Wynn had proposed to her after Sir John's funeral – and had been told that he would become her third husband, should Sir Richard die. Wynn himself died in 1580.

Katheryn arranged for one of her Wynn stepdaughters, aged nine, to marry her eldest son by her first marriage, aged ten. After Wynn's death, she betrothed her own infant daughter by him to young Simon Thelwall, whose father Edward became Katheryn's fourth and final husband.

This oil painting is by Adriaen van Cronenburgh (1520-1604), and it is likely that it was painted in Antwerp. The skull, symbolic of mortality, often appears in sixteenth-century portraits. The painting was bought for Wales in 1957 with help from the Friends of the Museum.

Right: *Katheryn of Berain, 'The Mother of Wales'* (1568) by Adriaen van Cronenburgh.

AN° DNI 1568

Friends of the Museum.

The Friends of the National Museum of Wales Committee was formed in 1954. It aimed to purchase 'things of interest to Wales' that the Museum might otherwise lack the financial resources to acquire.

A successful membership drive followed and in 1955 the Committee made its first purchase – a set of Bronze Age artefacts costing £300. Later acquisitions ranged from a model of Richard Trevithick's first railway locomotive to an Augustus John portrait of fellow artist Sir Frank Brangwyn. Since then, the Friends have contributed more than £350,000.

By the 1980s the Friends' role had expanded with, for example, the employment of volunteer members as exhibition guides. In 1983 the Museum hosted the annual conference of the British Association of Friends of Museums, of which the Friends had been a founding members.

The 1990s saw a further growth in activities, notably in relation to curatorial work and practical help behind the scenes. Trips across the UK and abroad featured prominently as did lectures with guest speakers. In 1996, an award-winning newsletter was introduced.

It might be thought invidious to single out individuals, but Miss Pat Kernick has a record of unparalleled distinction. She first served on the Committee in 1955, has chaired the Friends and, as Honorary President, remains active to this day in the affairs of the Friends.

Today, the Friends continue to generate a varied programme of members' events as well as providing support and acting as ambassadors for the Museum.

Left: Gilded iron gates at the gardens of St Fagans, restored with support from the Friends.

39
TNY

A recording project is launched to preserve oral history.

In 1957, St Fagans began to collect sound recordings of Welsh oral history, traditions and dialects. The subject matter in what is now the Sound Archive includes architecture, agriculture, crafts, folk tales, music, traditional medicine, courtship customs and death and burial customs.

Almost three quarters of the Archive is in Welsh, as recording the Welsh language was one of the driving forces behind the early initiative. This was a direct response to concerns, particularly following the 1951 Census, that the language was dying out.

Early items include phonograph cylinder recordings by the pioneers of the Welsh Folk-Song Society from before the First World War and copper disc recordings of Welsh dialect speakers recorded by the University of Wales's Board of Celtic Studies in the 1930s. There are also copies of BBC recordings from the late 1930s, when it recorded the last Welsh speakers in border areas such as south-east Breconshire.

Most of the English-language recordings were made in south Pembrokeshire, the counties on the English border and the industrial parts of Glamorgan.

There are now over 10,000 field recordings in the Archive. The sound recordings are carefully kept in the best possible environmental conditions and, in case of disaster, duplicate copies are stored at a remote site.

Left and above: Mr Llewellyn Evans (left) from mid-Wales being recorded for the Sound Archive.

An expert modeller retires, leaving a fabulous legacy.

1957 - 1967

The Museum has become renowned for its model-making expertise and its collection of botanical wax models helped found this reputation.

The Museum has more than 1,300 botanical models. The collection portrays the flora of Wales as well as specimens from Britain, Europe and the rest of the world. The majority of the models are made from beeswax, which when used skillfully produces a life-like quality. Dried botanical specimens can lose colour, shape and texture and are therefore of limited use for display and educational purposes. The use of wax models enables a scientifically accurate representation of rare or even extinct plant material in all seasons.

The collection has developed gradually since the Museum opened and is still growing today. Although some models were donated or bought from other institutions, many were made by botanical artists employed by the Museum. Their skills and techniques over the years gives the collection a vivid sense of diversity and historical value.

Evelyn Jenkins began model making when the Museum opened in 1927 and went on to make 487 models. After 32 years of wax model making, she retired in 1959 and remains the largest contributor to the Museum's collection. She passed on her skills to Roy Herbert who took over her post in 1959 and made models of exceptional quality. By retirement in 1982, he had produced 153 models.

Left and above: Models of fungi and flora.

A passion for painting benefits the nation.

By the end of her colourful life, Margaret Davies (1884-1963) wasn't just collecting art for herself – she was collecting for Wales. Some works even by-passed her home entirely and went straight into the national collections.

Margaret Sidney Davies was the younger of the Davies sisters of Gregynog in mid-Wales. Both sisters loved the arts throughout their lives. Margaret's first purchase of a work of art came in 1906 – the water colour *An Algerian* by the the Paris-born English painter Hercules Brabazon Brabazon.

Like her sister Gwendoline, Margaret collected many important works of French Impressionism. Among these was *At Bougival* by Berthe Morisot, the best-known female Impressionist. This painting hung for a time in Margaret's bedroom at Gregynog. Her collection also included works by Monet, Daumier, Manet and Sisley, as well as Pissarro's *Sunset at Rouen* and *Pont neuf, snow effect.*

By 1948, Gwendoline had stopped collecting art, but Margaret turned her attention to British contemporary art, acquiring works by Wyndham Lewis, Eric Gill, Stanley Spencer and Sir Kyffin Williams. She also bought a group of eighteenth-century views of Wales by Moses Griffiths and numerous drawings and watercolours by Augustus John, JD Innes, John Piper, Paul Nash and Josef Herman. A trained artist herself, Margaret's taste was possibly broader than her sister's.

It was generally accepted, following Gwendoline's bequest, that Margaret's collection was also destined for the Museum. Consequently, in the 1950s she sometimes bought with the advice of the Museum, and rounded off her collection with some semi-abstract works, which did not necessarily reflect her own personal taste. In fact, some of Margaret's last purchases were sent straight to the Museum, for instance the watercolour *Landscape with Bonfire* by the Austrian artist Oscar Kokoschka.

Left: *The Palazzo Dario* (1908) by Claude Monet.
Above: *At Bougival* (1882) by Berthe Morisot.

Gwendoline and Margaret Davies amassed one of the great British art collections of the twentieth century. Brought up in a strict Nonconformist Welsh tradition, the sisters believed strongly in using their immense wealth to improve the lives of others. They wanted to give the people of Wales the chance to learn and improve themselves through the arts. This, coupled with their visionary and pioneering art collecting, led to two outstanding bequests that would completely transform the Welsh national art collection.

The Davies sisters of Gregynog, a lifetime of philanthropy.

The sisters were the grand-daughters of David Davies of Llandinam, who built the family fortune from mining and railways in the Industrial Revolution.

During the First World War, they ran Red Cross canteens for the French troops. They and their brother David were major benefactors of a range of charities and cultural institutions in Wales. In 1920, they bought Gregynog Hall, near Newtown, in order to create a centre of artistic creativity. There, they set up the Gregynog Press. In 1932, they established the Gregynog Music Festival, attracting leading figures such as Vaughan Williams and Gustav Holst. In the Second World War, Gregynog was used as a convalescent home.

From 1908, they began avidly collecting art. Their governess Jane Blaker introduced them to her brother, the critic and dealer Hugh Blaker. He was instrumental in helping them with their purchases, and encouraged their pioneering support of modern French art. By 1924 they had built up one of the largest and most important collections of French Impressionist and Post-Impressionist works in the country. Their collection also includes Richard Wilson, Turner and many works by Augustus John.

Much of the Davies family legacy can still be seen today, for example the Temple of Peace in Cardiff, the beautiful Gregynog Press books in the Museum's Library and, of course, the Museum's stunning art collection.

Above: Gwendoline (left) and Margaret Davies.
Right: *Provençal Landscape* (1888) by Paul Cézanne.

The Museum buys an eighteenth-century toilet service fit for a queen.

In the eighteenth century, a toilet service would usually comprise a table mirror, casket, boxes – including a puff box – brushes, a ewer and basin and lighting devices such as candlesticks and snuffers. The number of items depended on the rank of the lady.

Sir Watkin Williams-Wynn (1749-1789), one of Britain's wealthiest eighteenth-century landowners, was a great patron of the arts. Based in north Wales, he did not confine his admiration of fine things to paintings alone. This intricate toilet service, in the elaborately ornamental style of the period, was crafted for his marriage in 1769 to Lady Henrietta Somerset, daughter of the Fourth Duke of Beaufort. The service was a gift from his mother to her new daughter-in-law.

At this time the range of pieces in a toilet service was growing, reflecting the increasing complexity of cosmetic devices becoming available. Such services would also contain showy items for display, as fashionable ladies would receive morning visitors in their dressing rooms.

This service was made by the royal goldsmith, Thomas Heming, in silver gilt. It is hallmarked London 1768-9 and bears the arms of Sir Watkin and his bride. Tragically, she died three months after their marriage.

Eighteen pieces in this service are nearly identical to items in a service made by Heming as a gift from King George III to his youngest sister Princess Caroline Matilda on her marriage to Christian VII of Denmark in 1766. Both sets are decorated in the Rococo style, an ornate mix of scrolls and shellwork more widespread on the Continent than in Britain.

The toilet service was bought by the Museum in 1964 with the support of the Art Fund.

Left and above: The silver gilt toilet service (1768-9) by Thomas Heming, London.

A dedicated collector forms an important Jurassic collection.

James Frederick Jackson collected fossils of all types and sizes. The only restriction was whether or not he could carry his specimen home. His interests and exploits eventually benefited the Museum's geological collections, with nearly 21,000 rocks, fossils and minerals, as well as photographs, maps and publications.

Jackson was born in Mold, north Wales in 1894 but moved to Hunstanton, Norfolk when he was a child. This was where he first took part in geological forays along the cliffs, aged six or seven.

In 1908 he was seen collecting geological specimens by Bellerby Lowerison, Principal of the nearby Ruskin School, who was fascinated by the young boy's knowledge. Lowerison encouraged Jackson to write an account of the local geology in a small book and gathered financial support from local businesses in the form of advertisements. The book, *The Rocks of Hunstanton and its Neighbourhood*, was published in 1910 and caught the attention of geologists, including Frederick J. North, who worked at the Museum and later became its first keeper of geology.

When a post arose for a general assistant in the Department of Geology in 1914, Jackson was encouraged by North to apply. He got the job and moved to south Wales where he collected widely both officially and in his own time. At the end of 1923, Jackson sold the remainder of his private collections, many to the Museum, and moved to the Isle of Wight.

Jackson maintained regular correspondence with North and continuously sent collections to the Museum. His Jurassic fossils form an extremely important part of the Museum's geological collections, and are consulted regularly by visiting specialists in Jurassic geology.

At the end of his life, Jackson lived in Charmouth, in the company of his numerous cats. When he died in 1966, he requested that half the money raised from the sale of his modest estate should go to the Museum, and the rest to the People's Dispensary for Sick Animals.

**Far left: Pentacrinites fossils.
Left: Promicroceras planicosta.
Above: James Frederick Jackson in his later years with Peter, the favourite amongst his many cats.**

A rock from the Moon is exhibited in Cardiff – and attracts almost 10,000 visitors in one day.

1967-1977

Study of the specimens that astronauts brought back from the Moon allowed scientists, for the first time, to investigate the geological history of another world.

In December 1969, museum visitors queued round the block to see a sample of rock brought back from the Moon by Apollo 11. Rocks from the Moon are extremely old compared to those on Earth. They range in age from about 3.2 billion years up to about 4.5 billion years old, whereas the Earth's oldest rocks date from about 3.9 billion years. Older formations have been destroyed and recycled by the constant shifting of the Earth's tectonic plates.

Today, a piece of Moon rock from the Apollo 12 mission, on loan from NASA, is on display as part of the exhibition *The Evolution of Wales* at National Museum Cardiff. It is kept in a special airtight container filled with nitrogen to protect it from contamination. At 3.3 billion years old, it is considerably older than the most ancient Welsh rock, which is displayed alongside it – and a mere 702 million years old.

Left: A sample of rock brought back from the moon.
Above: Visitors queue round the block to see the lunar sample.

Evidence of historic Welsh traditions go on display.

The first galleries at St Fagans displayed some unusual and attractive exhibits. They ranged from corn dollies and lovespoons to burial stockings, worn on the body after death, and homemade valentine offerings.

St Fagans opened as a ground-breaking open-air museum in 1948 and went on to display a fascinating selection of re-erected buildings. In 1970, the Gallery of Material Culture opened in the main visitor building. On display were objects from the Museum's social and cultural history collections that could not be shown in the re-erected houses.

Four years later, St Fagans added the Agricultural Gallery. As well as displaying examples of carts, sheds and farm wagons, this gallery traced the farming year from hedging and ditching through ploughing and planting to harvest. Photographs show farming techniques from different parts of Wales, and a section on livestock includes a comprehensive collection of veterinary equipment.

In 1976, the Costume and Textile Gallery opened. Due to the delicate nature of many materials this gallery is kept cool and dimly lit to reduce the risk of fading and damage from pests. A selection of quilts and patchwork items shows the skills of Welsh women through two hundred years. There are also embroideries and samplers, many of which were made by children.

Exhibits from the Gallery of Material Culture can now be seen in the innovative new Oriel 1 Gallery.

Above: A garment from the Costume Gallery.
Right: A Welsh alphabet chart, devised by T. C. Evans, c. 1900.

Y WYDDOR (The Alphabet)
A a
AFAL APPLE
B b
BARDD BARD
C c
CATH CAT
Ch ch
CHWILEN BEETLE
D d
DERWYDD DRUID
Dd dd
EI DDEFAID HIS SHEEP
E e
ERYR EAGLE
F f
Y FEGIN THE BELLOWS
Ff ff
FFWLBART POLECAT
G g
GAFR GOAT
Ng ng
FY NGHEFFYL MY HORSE
H h
HIRLAS DRINKING HORN
I i
IAR HEN
L l
DAU LEW TWO LIONS
Ll ll
LLWYNOG FOX
M m
MWYALCH BLACKBIRD
N n
NYTH NEST
O o
OEN LAMB
P p
PAUN PEACOCK
Ph ph
MELIN A PHONT MILL & BRIDGE
R r
ROBIN GOCH
Rh rh
RHAW SHOVEL
S s
SACH SACK
T t
TARIAN SHIELD
Th th
A THELYN AND A HARP
U u
UCHEDYDD LARK
W w
WYAU EGGS
Y y
YCHAIN OXEN
Letters upon stone Monuments in Wales 6th to 10 Centuries.
THE BETHLUISNION. (OGHAM ALPHABET)
b l f s n h d t c p m g ng st r a o u e i ea oi ui ia ae
COELBREN Y BEIRDD.
a b c ch d dd e f ff g
ng h i l ll m n nh o p
ph r rh s t th u w wh y
Letters upon stone Monuments in Wales 6th to 10 Centuries.

The British Bryological Society Herbarium arrives at the Museum.

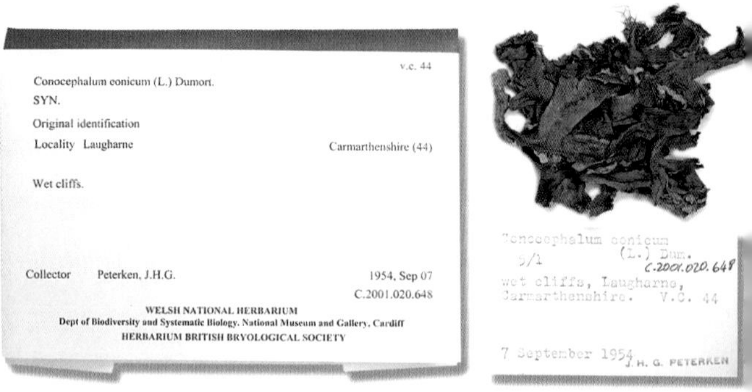

The British Bryological Society, with an international membership, is Britain's leading organization for the study of mosses and liverworts. In 1970, its collection was loaned to the Museum.

The British Bryological Society's collection of 35,000 specimens brought the total holdings for the Museum's Cryptogamic Herbarium to more than 330,000 specimens. The Museum's complete bryological collection is the second largest in the UK, behind only the Natural History Museum. The herbarium is a significant centre for the study of mosses and liverworts.

In 2001, ownership of the collection was transferred to the Museum. This allowed much-needed conservation of the specimens, many of which were in poor condition. They were packeted in a range of different materials, as they had been donated to the collection by a wide variety of people. As the specimens are relatively small and dry, they are particularly fragile. Curation work at the Museum allows repacketing in high quality materials to protect the specimens for the future.

Above: A dried specimen of the liverwort *Conocephalum conicum.*
Right: An enlarged image of a ventral scale from *Conocephalum conicum.*

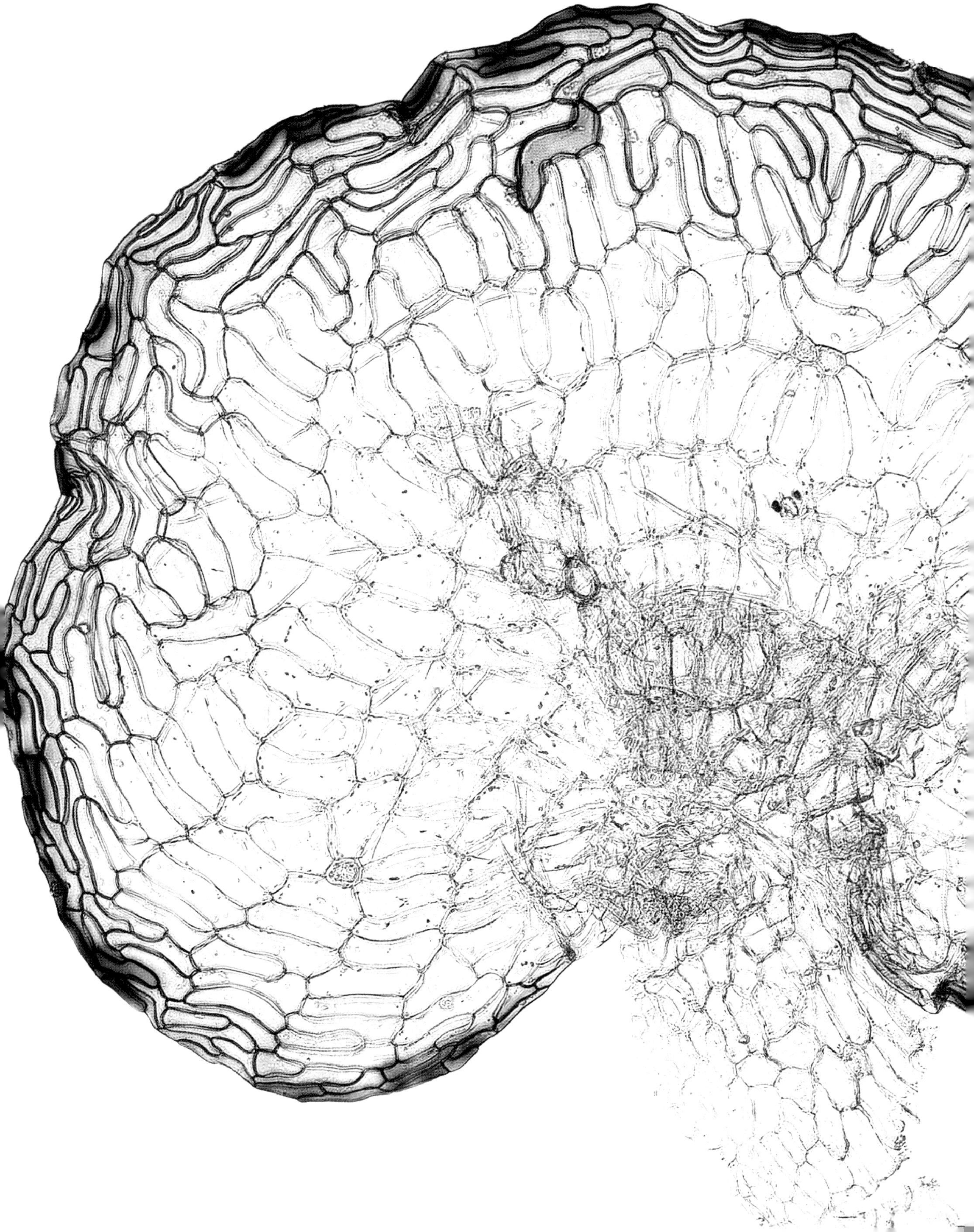

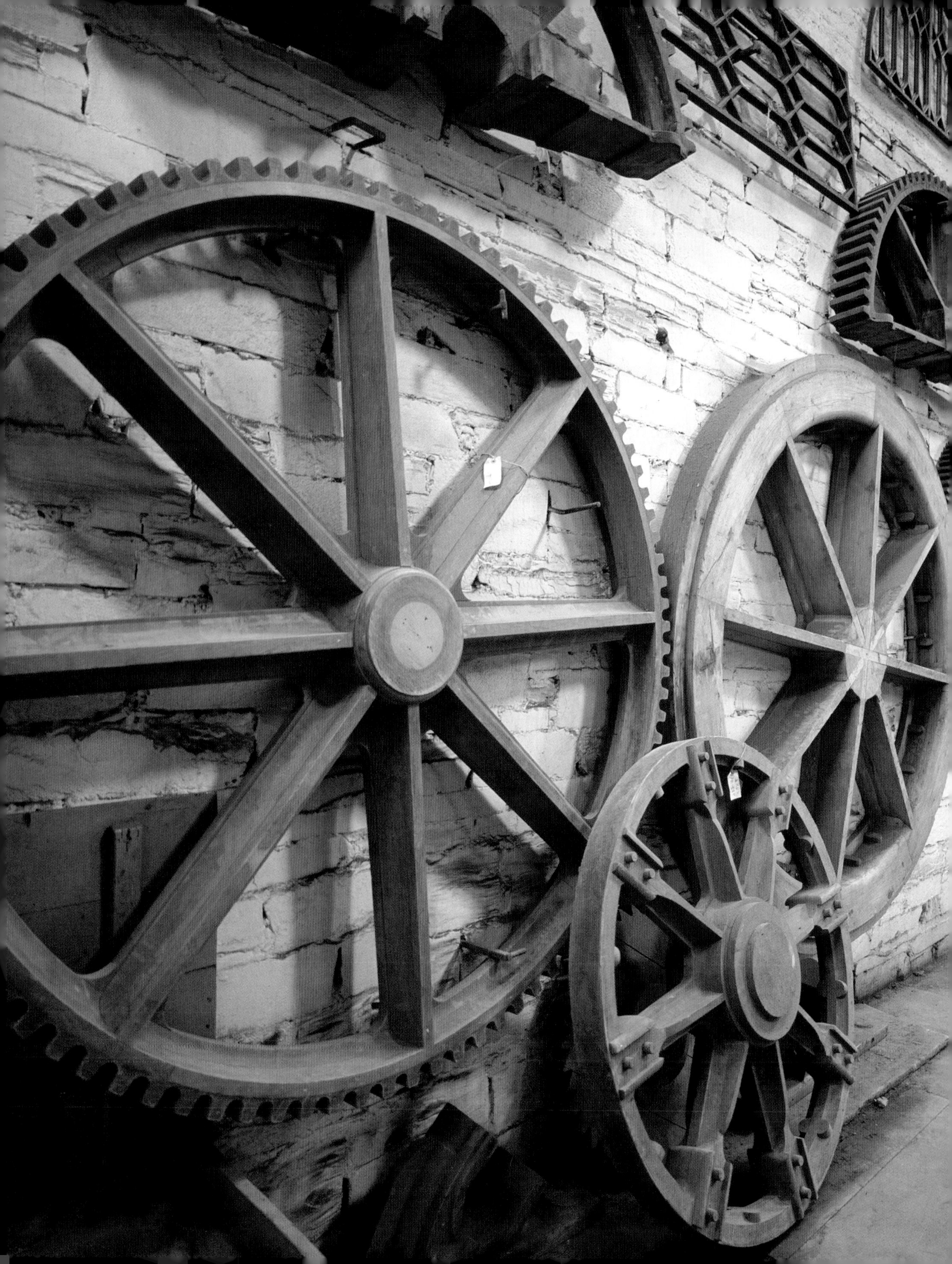

Powerful memories of danger-filled human endeavour are kept alive as the National Slate Museum opens.

The late 1960s saw gloom in the once powerful north Wales slate business as work and jobs drained away. However, the efforts of the people who made the industry great were not to be forgotten.

Left and above right: Inside the Pattern Loft at the National Slate Museum.
Above: Drawing of the National Slate Museum by Sir Kyffin Williams.

In the eighteenth century the north Wales slate quarries formed a true industrial powerhouse. However, the twentieth century saw a gradual erosion in fortunes.

The three-year Penrhyn Strike of the early 1900s greatly affected the whole of north Wales, with many customers turning to other suppliers. The Second World War badly affected demand for slate, and the industry never fully recovered. In August 1969, Dinorwig Quarry suddenly closed.

Luckily for future generations, there was acknowledgment that the memory should live on. Many items were saved from the auctioneer's hammer by the sterling efforts of a few former workers, particularly Hugh Richard Jones, the former Chief Engineer.

In 1972, the National Slate Museum opened to the public, with Hugh Richard Jones as manager. Many of the site's former quarrymen and engineers were employed to present and interpret their craft. Significant examples of equipment were collected, often from other Welsh quarries.

In later years the quarry's incline was restored to its former glory, with the help of an award from the Heritage Lottery Fund (HLF). It is now the only working incline in Britain. HLF money also made possible radical redevelopment, and the National Slate Museum re-opened in 1999 with unique features and facilities that offer an unparalleled day out in the richly wooded lakeside landscape of Padarn Country Park.

The Museum is designed as though the quarrymen and engineers have just put down their tools and left the workshops for home. With imaginative interpretation, the remarkable relics of the slate industry can be understood and enjoyed by children and adults alike. Visitors can enjoy slate-splitting demonstrations and a fascinating tour of the workshops and water-powered machinery that manufactured the tools for quarrying slate.

In 2005, the Museum scooped the Wales Tourist Board's prestigious 'Sense of Place Award' and is regularly cited by the HLF as a good example of well-structured development.

An industrial powerhouse that once helped to 'roof the world'.

Great explosions once freed hundreds of tons of slate from the rock at Dinorwig Quarry. Inevitably, there were numerous deaths and injuries – and this meant that welfare and the community were crucial aspects of life.

The Industrial Revolution saw slate became one of Wales's major industries. The country would eventually produce over four-fifths of all British slate, with Caernarfonshire the biggest producing county in Wales.

The 'Great New Quarry' of Dinorwig was founded in 1788. It belonged to the wealthy landowning family of Assheton Smith, whose estate, Y Faenol, on the banks of the Menai Straits, covered 34,000 acres. By the 1870s Dinorwig Quarry employed more than 3,000 people. In 1898, the slate industry in Wales reached its peak, with 17,000 men producing 485,000 tons of slate.

Working life, however, was dangerous. Between 1822 and 1969, 362 men were killed at Dinorwig. In 1860 a hospital was built so that injured or sick quarrymen, or any family member who fell ill, could be treated there. Long before the Welfare State, the 'hospital shilling' (5p) was kept back from the men's pay to fund the hospital.

The quarry workers gathered during their breaks in the *Caban*, to socialise and to discuss current affairs. The *Caban's* president would read aloud from newspapers and announce details of local events such as concerts and special chapel services. It was an honour to be elected president – it meant that the men greatly respected your wisdom and integrity. *Eisteddfodau* would be held with all sorts of competitions, from solo recitations to ambulance teams.

The men sat in a strict order around a stove with the youngest boys closest to the door, and the *ffowntan* (fountain), as the tea-urn was called, would be on constant simmer.

Dinorwig Quarry had all the repair and maintenance back-up needed from the engineers of Gilfach Ddu workshops. They prided themselves that they could build or mend any piece of equipment needed. The workshops included three sawing sheds, each with specialist saws for different types of work, iron and brass foundries and forges. The water wheel – 15.4 metres across – supplied energy to the workshops until 1925. It remains the largest working water wheel on mainland Britain.

The notorious Penrhyn Strike of 1900-1903 greatly affected the whole north Wales slate trade, with many customers turning to other suppliers. The Second World War reduced the demand for slate, and the industry was never to fully recover. In August 1969, without warning, Dinorwig Quarry closed. The powerhouse had run out of steam.

Above and right (bottom): The workers of Dinorwig Quarry. Right (top): Splitting and dressing slates.

A dramatic rescue mission saves some of Wales's most impressive industrial artefacts.

Dinorwig Quarry's sudden closure in 1969 was a shattering blow to the local community. However, the spirit of the quarry workers and their families survived, as exemplified by the quarry's former Chief Engineer, Hugh Richard Jones. He led an ambitious initiative to rescue many of its tools and machinery from the scrap yard. Three years later he became the first manager of the National Slate Museum.

Jones began work at Dinorwig quarry in 1926, aged just fifteen years old. He started out as an apprentice, working grueling twelve-hour days. Like all apprentices, his first six months of work were unpaid until his skills were perfected.

After the Second World War, life at the quarry altered considerably. Many quarrymen had enlisted in the army and the demand for building slates fell drastically. However, the quarry continued working until its sudden closure in 1969.

The equipment and fittings were all put up for auction. When Jones saw that the magnificent water wheel was about to be burned for scrap, he stepped in. He wanted to save it, as a valuable reminder of a great industry. With the help of his friends he sent away the auctioneers and rescued many items from the scrap yard.

He saw these pieces as 'raw materials for a splendid museum' and, with others, spent three years persuading the council to buy the old buildings and surrounding land, the Department of the Environment to care for them and the Museum to take control. When the National Slate Museum opened in 1972, Jones was employed as its first manager. It received 36,000 visitors in its first season, and has since gone from strength to strength.

In 1983, Jones was awarded the British Empire Medal and congratulated by the Queen for his twenty-four years of dedication to the quarry. He died in 2001, aged eighty-nine.

**Left: The water wheel at the National Slate Museum – now the largest working example on mainland Britain.
Above: Hugh Richard Jones.**

Art's supertalented siblings.

Gwen and Augustus John were as different as brother and sister could be. One moved abroad, one stayed in the UK. Gwen became a recluse. Augustus enjoyed increasing numbers of patrons. Their art differed too, but both are represented at the Museum.

In 1976, part of Gwen John's studio collection arrived in Cardiff. It added nearly 1,000 drawings to the Museum's collection of Augustus and Gwen's work.

Gwen was born in 1876, Augustus eighteen months later. They both progressed to London's Slade School of Art. By 1899 Augustus was attracting considerable attention due to both his skill and his Bohemian lifestyle. That year he held his first one-man show at London's New English Art Club. Gwen also lived in London and in 1903 they exhibited together. However, by the following year she had settled in Paris, where she later met Rodin. She modelled for him and became his mistress. After Rodin's death in 1917, Gwen became a recluse.

Gwen's work consisted almost entirely of small-scale portraits and still-lifes. Although well known early in the twentieth century for his drawing and etching, the bulk of Augustus's later work consisted of portrait commissions. He was particularly known for the psychological insight of his portraits, which some considered almost cruel. Lord Leverhulme was so upset about his that he cut out the head.

Though Gwen was once overshadowed by her brother, critical opinion now tends to view her as the more talented. She painted slowly, preferring reduced tone and subtle colour relationships, in contrast to her brother's far more vivid palette.

After Gwen's death in 1939, Augustus claimed that fifty years after his death he would be remembered as Gwen John's brother and, indeed, during the past twenty years Gwen's reputation has soared. She is now acclaimed as a major painter, perhaps even Britain's finest Impressionist. After Augustus's death in 1961, the Museum bought much of the contents of his studio.

Left: *Girl in hat, facing right* by Gwen John.
Above: Portrait of Gwen (c. 1900) by Ambrose McEvoy and self portrait of Augustus (1913).

Constructing a purpose-built public attraction – the first new museum building since before the war, and the first new building in Cardiff's docklands since the 1920s – would be a challenge. It wasn't made any easier by the fact that the development would take place in an area where dereliction was becoming rampant.

An award-winning new building houses the motive power of Welsh industry.

The architecture of the new Welsh Industrial & Maritime Museum was strongly influenced by the nation's industrial themes – and by the operational requirements of displaying very large objects. In fact, the artefacts to be displayed were so large that the new structure had to be built around them after they had been installed.

This building, called the Hall of Power, was intended to be the first of a number of galleries built in the immediate area, but the plans were constantly modified as dockland redevelopment quickened in the late 1980s.

Above: *Devonia* by W. D. England.

The new building – opened in 1977 – contained a number of massive industrial machines, such as a beam engine that had once pumped clean water for Cardiff, a colliery haulage engine and a massive colliery fan engine that had once ventilated a mine at Crumlin, near Newbridge. Examples of smaller steam engines and internal combustion engines were to be found on a mezzanine floor.

Vessels including a tug, a pilot cutter and a lifeboat stood in the old West Bute basin, and nearby there were vehicles ranging from a traction engine to a Sinclair C5, from a penny farthing to examples of the only Welsh-made car – the Gilbern. A programme of temporary exhibitions displayed smaller artefacts, ranging from ship models to miners' lamps, while a fine collection of pictures of Welsh industrial scenes and a massive photographic archive of more than 100,000 images was built up over the years.

Massive changes to the post-war workplace inspire a new opportunity for museum visitors.

The historic industries of Wales underwent radical changes during the second half of the twentieth century. The older, male-dominated heavy industries went into decline, to be replaced by lighter hi-tech factories where women often made up the majority of the workforce. At the same time, industrial archaeology emerged as a new discipline. Museum staff explored how best they could tackle this area of our heritage and, in 1959, the Department of Industry was established.

Above left: A working replica of Richard Trevithick's steam locomotive, which can now be seen at the National Waterfront Museum.
Above right: An aerial view of the Welsh Industrial & Maritime Museum, in the top left of the photograph.

The development of many Welsh industries had been studied up to the 1950s by the Museum's Geology Department. Its keeper, Frederick J. North, was deeply interested in what he called 'economic geology', particularly the extractive industries such as coal and slate.

These collections would come to be complemented by the artefacts and photographs collected by the Department of Industry. New galleries to display and interpret the industrial collections (including a mock-up of a coal mine, for long a great favourite) were opened in the west wing of National Museum Cardiff in 1967.

With the pace of industrial change quickening, the Department of Industry collected and recorded in the fields of industry, maritime trade and land transport. However, a number of large machines saved from closing collieries and factories were too big to display in the Department's galleries at Cathays Park.

By the early 1970s the idea of establishing 'an industrial St Fagans' was under consideration. A site was eventually found around the West Bute basin, appropriately in the heart of Cardiff's historic dockland, and the new museum – The Welsh Industrial & Maritime Museum – was opened by the then Prime Minister James Callaghan in 1977.

1977 - 1987

The Neanderthals of Pontnewydd Cave.

Excavations at Pontnewydd Cave in Denbighshire between 1978 and 1995 uncovered Wales's oldest known human remains. They dated back 230,000 years and are possibly one of the earliest examples of deliberate disposal of the dead. These early Neanderthals left traces of crude stone tools, animal bones and their own bones and teeth.

Nineteen human teeth were found deep inside Pontnewydd Cave. They had been washed by melt water from a melting ice cap that had covered much of Wales. They were identified by experts from the Natural History Museum, London as belonging to an early form of Neanderthal.

Neanderthals are thought to have died out around 30,000 years ago. We share a common ancestor with them, but we did not evolve from Neanderthals. They were short and stocky, with big square jaws, heavy brow ridges and larger teeth than our own.

The teeth at Pontnewydd Cave are from at least five individuals. The individuals range in age from young children to adults. The most complete discovery is a fragment of the upper jaw of a child who died aged around eight. A heavily worn milk tooth sits next to a new permanent molar (see below).

The animal bones are from cave bear, horse, roe deer, red deer, various rhinoceros species, lions and leopards. Stone tools were found in the cave, and cut marks made by these early hunters are visible on cave bear and horse bones. Dating to a much later period, bones and teeth of classic glacial animals were also found here, including wolf, reindeer, horse and lemming. This indicates that the Welsh climate became very cold again 30,000 years ago, possibly similar to Scandinavia today. Bones of birds that now spend their summers in the Arctic, only visiting the Welsh estuaries and marshes in winter, were also found. They would have shared the skies with eagles, buzzards, choughs, capercaillies and snowy owls.

Questions remain as to whether these humans were originally buried in graves in the cave. Unfortunately, the forces that remarkably preserved the remains also destroyed any evidence of their original burial conditions.

Left: The entrance to Pontnewydd Cave.
Above: The interior of the cave.
Right: Teeth from the oldest human remains known in Wales, excavated at Pontnewydd Caves.

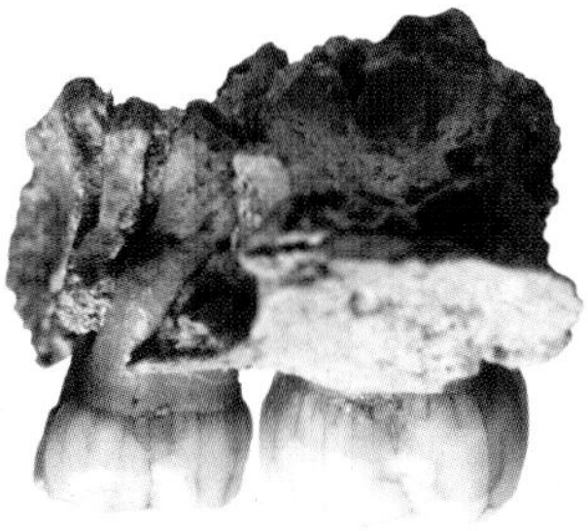

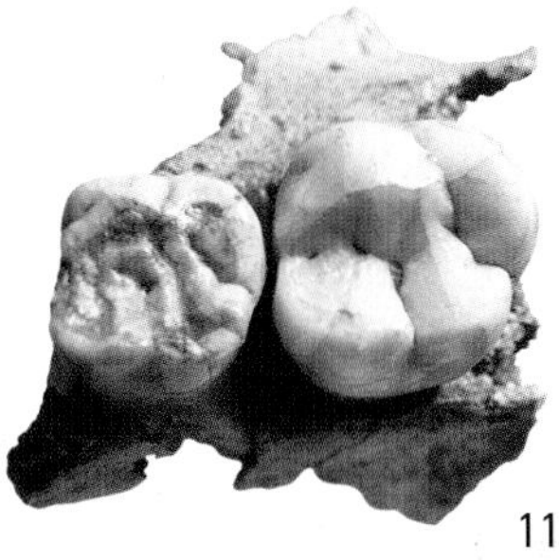

One of the largest gemstone collections found anywhere in the Roman Empire is discovered.

As highly skilled craftsmen worked on their gems, they weren't to realise that the future of these precious artefacts would involve more than 1,700 years languishing down a drain.

This splendid collection of 88 engraved gemstones was discovered beneath the remains of Caerleon's Roman baths – lost by Roman bathers, during the lifetime of the baths, between AD 80 and AD 230.

Most had probably been brought from far afield. Much raw material for Roman gem cutting centres originated in Cyprus, Egypt, India or Sri Lanka. Caerleon's gems are engraved with a range of deities, personifications and symbols. They were the product of extremely talented craftsmen who worked on a minute scale without the aid of magnification. A range of semi-precious stones, mostly varieties of quartz, was used for engraving.

They would originally have been set in finger-rings, and served as signets and charms or talismans for their owners. Most would have belonged to soldiers, but some might have been lost by the civilians and women who were allowed to use the baths.

Once lost, they remained so for centuries. They were only rediscovered as the fortress baths were being excavated in 1979. Although excavation had taken place at the legionary fortress since 1926, the baths were not discovered until the mid-sixties and their exploration was not complete until 1981.

The gemstones are now on show at the National Roman Legion Museum.

Left and above: Intricately carved gem stones found during the excavation of Roman baths in Caerleon.

Eight hundred year-old coins are discovered buried in a Welsh woodland.

The Coed-y-Wenallt hoard was found by metal detectorists in the summer of 1980 in the woodland north of Cardiff. The coins are from the time of King Stephen, who reigned over England from 1135 to 1154. They are thought to have been buried in the early 1140s. Months after their discovery, the 102 silver pennies were declared Treasure Trove at a coroner's inquest. They were valued at £103,040, and the Museum bought 34 of them.

Small and ill-struck they may have been, but the brittle Coed-y-Wenallt discs were a sensational find. They suddenly trebled the number of known coins of the Empress Matilda.

The only living child of King Henry I, Matilda (1101-1169) was the legitimate heir to the English throne. But when Henry died in 1135, Matilda was in Anjou, western France. Her ambitious cousin Stephen hurried to England from Boulogne – and was crowned King of England.

The year 1138 saw the outbreak of civil war, and this period became known as The Anarchy. Matilda and Stephen set up rival courts in Bristol and London and issued their own coinage from the mints under their control. Matilda's currency was minted at Bristol, Cardiff, Oxford and Wareham in Dorset.

Until February 1141, Matilda's coins carried her own title but bore the same heraldic cross moline as those of Stephen. However, after she was victorious in battle at Lincoln, a new coinage was struck with variations of a cross plumée over a saltire fleury. This was a coinage unknown to modern historians before the discovery at Coed-y-Wenallt, which was largely composed of coins from Matilda's Cardiff mint, hitherto extremely rare.

Silver pennies were the only currency in Stephen's time and these were often simply cut into halves or quarters for lower coin denominations. Some barons were given, or assumed, the right to strike coins in their own names. The Wenallt hoard included such coins struck for the Baron John of St John. It also included the first-known coins of a Swansea mint, struck in the name of Baron Henry de Neubourg.

The civil war ended in 1153 when Stephen acknowledged Matilda's son, Henry, to be his successor to the throne.

Above: Penny of Henry de Neubourg, c. 1141.
Right: Pennies of the Empress Matilda, c. 1140.

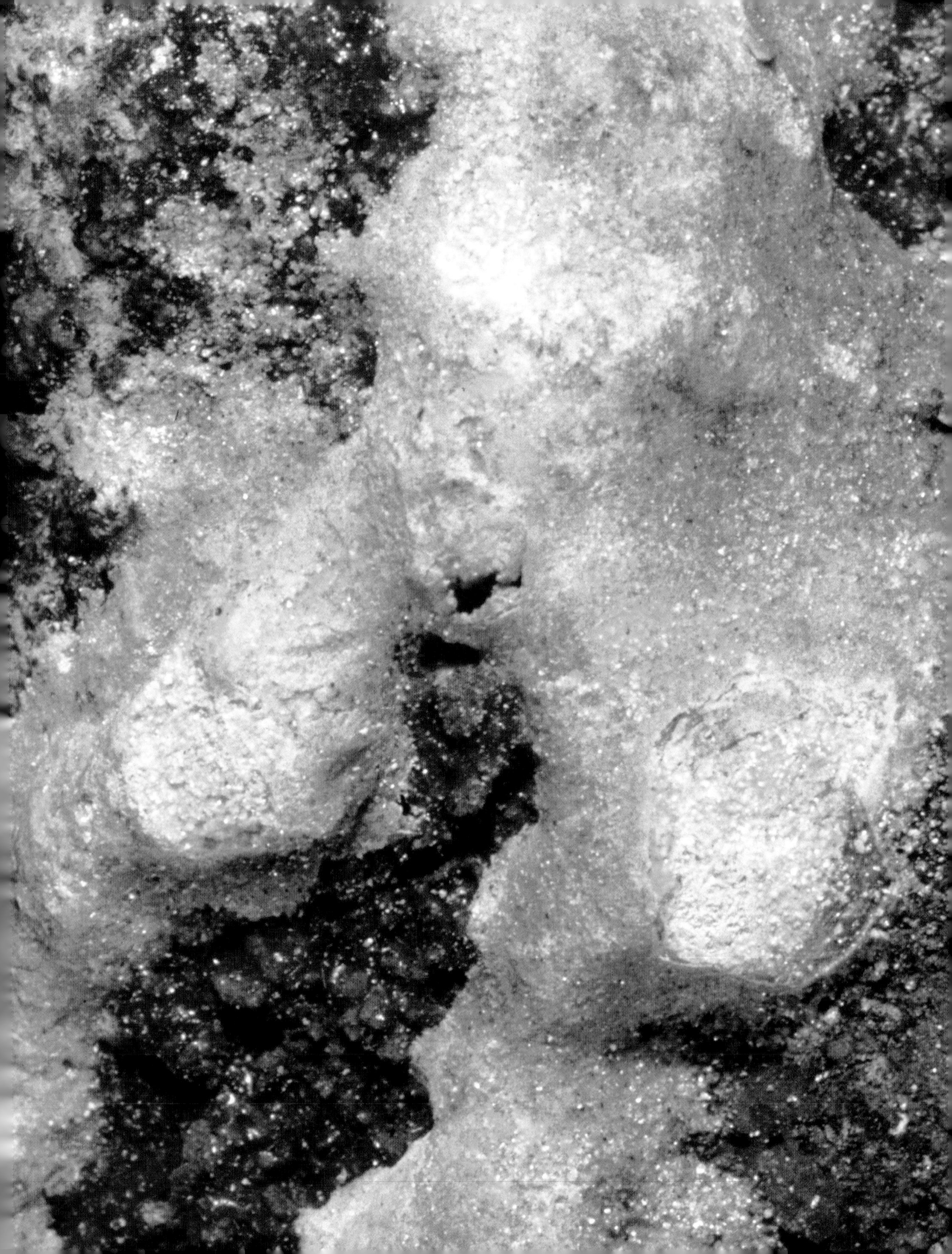

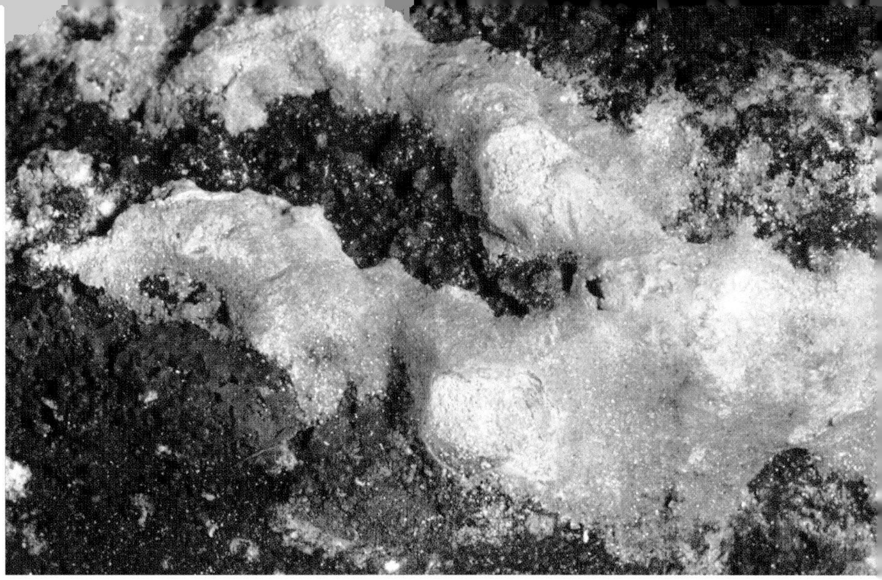

So when is hydrozincite not hydrozincite?

Only the diligence of Museum experts allowed the world to learn of a mineral that had never before been studied or catalogued.

The specimen had spent more than half a century in the Museum's care when, in 1981, it was chosen for further investigation. Bearing the label 'hydrozincite' it was pulled from the mineral collection for new study.

This item had originated in the Aberllyn Mine near Betws-y-Coed, north Wales, and was acquired by the Museum in 1927. But all was not as it seemed. Examination of the specimen cast doubt on the original identification and, after closer analysis, the team discovered that it was, in fact, a mineral species completely new to science. The new discovery was named namuwite, after the National Museum of Wales, and has since been recorded at more than twenty other sites worldwide.

This discovery is just one illustration of the important role the Museum plays in international academic scholarship worldwide. The Museum has many fields of expertise that are not well developed in universities, such as taxonomy and classification into specially named groups. A 'type specimen', like namuwite, is a specimen that is used as a benchmark for all future studies of that species, worldwide.

Left and above: Namuwite, a new mineral discovered by the Museum in its collections in 1981.

A hands-on stitch in time.

Visitors to the National Wool Museum can try their hand at spinning and sewing. It's just one way the Museum illustrates what life was like for those who once worked at the building in its days as a mill. Shirts and shawls, blankets and bedcovers, woollen stockings and socks were all made here and sold in the surrounding countryside – and to the rest of the world.

During the late 1800s and early part of the next century, the woollen industry sustained the Welsh rural community. Cambrian Mills, at Dre-fach Felindre in Carmarthenshire, was one of the largest woollen mills in west Wales. Having run a small gallery at the Mill since the mid-seventies, in 1984 the Museum purchased the whole site to create a national museum to tell the story of the industry and its people.

Today, the Museum recalls how people depended on spinning and weaving for their livelihood and exhibits national collections relating to the industry.

The mill buildings have been sympathetically restored. Old machinery, including the Whiteley Spinning Mule, has been brought back into working condition, and a new gallery presents aspects of the National Flat Textile Collection for the first time.

Other new features include a glass-roofed courtyard and a raised walkway that gives a unique view of textiles in production at Melin Teifi, the site's commercial woollen mill.

Left and right (top and bottom): Equipment and textiles on view today at the National Wool Museum.

A very Welsh industry.

By the time the former Cambrian Mills became a visitor attraction, it already had a long, distinguished history of employment and textile production.

Wales's woollen industry, pioneered by Cistercian monks, was one of the country's most important employers by the thirteenth century. But that was only the start. It was to become the most widespread of Welsh industries.

Huge expansion began with the arrival of the power loom in 1850. The Teifi Valley in west Wales had the largest concentration of the country's woollen mills, with the area within five miles of Dre-fach Felindre seeing twenty-one factories built between 1860 and the end of the century. The trade found a ready market in south Wales as the mines and steelworks prospered.

The Teifi Valley factories produced much fine flannel for shirts. Other products included blankets, tweeds and yarn. Typically, they employed between fifty and a hundred people and were situated near road or rail links.

It was at Dre-fach Felindre in 1902 that the first Cambrian Mills was established. David Lewis built it on the site of a small water-powered weaving workshop at Doldywyll ('Dark Meadow'), on land rented from the Llysnewydd Estate. He was from a well known and respected local family, which already owned many of Teifi Valley's large mills.

First built was a south-facing mill. Its remains are concealed within today's L- shaped building. Little is known about this early structure, but the mill race that drove its machinery later served a new Cambrian Mills. The building was damaged by fire in 1919, and although it was rebuilt, it no longer had its original third storey.

David Lewis ran the Mill until he retired in 1921, aged 75. His son, Johnny, took over.

Left: The looms of Cambrian Mills.
Above: Sorting the wool.

A Cardiff-based arts trust reveals how painter Michael Andrews took a pilgrimage to his personal cathedral.

Above: *The Cathedral, the Southern Faces / Uluru (Ayers Rock)* (1987) by Michael Andrews. Derek Williams Trust on loan to Amgueddfa Cymru – National Museum Wales.

Chartered surveyor Derek Williams (1929-1984) was an enthusiastic private collector of art. Since his death, the Derek Williams Trust has continued to develop the collection he founded. The Trust works with the Museum, which houses the collection, to acquire contemporary art. *The Cathedral, the Southern Faces / Uluru (Ayers Rock)* was the Trust's first addition to the collection.

Michael Andrews (1928-1995) was born in Norwich and studied at London's Slade School of Art. From 1959 he taught at Slade and the Chelsea School of Art. Though Andrews did not exhibit widely during his lifetime, he was regarded as one of the late twentieth century's great painters of portraits and modern conversation pieces.

In 1983 he fulfilled a longstanding ambition to visit Uluru, or Ayers Rock. Andrews saw his journey as something of a pilgrimage and he was moved by the Rock's ancient aboriginal significance as a spiritual site.

Back in Norfolk, Andrews made an ambitious series of large paintings of the Rock and the surrounding landscape. These paintings were based on the numerous watercolours and photographs he had taken on the spot. In his paintings he alludes to the Rock's dual significance as religious site and tourist attraction by the contrast between the profound subject matter and the bright colours and flat handling, reminiscent of Pop Art.

Painted in 1987, this monumental picture, along with other works from the Trust, is on long-term loan to the Museum.

A private art collector ensures that many wonderful works are where he wanted them to be – on public view.

Derek Williams (1929-1984) derived enormous satisfaction from building his collection of twentieth-century British art. A chartered surveyor in his family's practice, Williams began buying art in the 1960s, mainly from the Howard Roberts Gallery in Cardiff. Roberts recalls the first painting he sold to his new client – a Ceri Richards drawing, bought as a gift for a friend.

For over ten years, Williams regularly visited Roberts' exhibitions. He bought more than two-thirds of his collection there and was particularly drawn to John Piper landscapes. The twenty-one Piper paintings and drawings that he eventually owned constitute the largest and finest group in his collection. In 1965 Williams made his most significant purchase – the preparatory sketch for Stanley Spencer's *Resurrection, Cookham*.

On his death in 1984, Williams left more than seventy pictures, and his personal fortune became the basis of the Derek Williams Trust. The collection featured artists such as Lucien Freud, David Jones, Henry Moore and Ben Nicholson. More than half the works in his collection were by Welsh artists or artists with strong links to Wales.

Today, the Trust's funds are used to make additions to the collection, which is on long-term loan to the Museum, and to acquire works in partnership with the Museum and other national bodies.

**Left: *Dragon's pot* by Ceri Richards. Derek Williams Trust on loan to Amgueddfa Cymru – National Museum Wales.
Above: Derek Williams**

FOR GEORGE VI
OUR EMPEROR KING,
THE BELLS THROUGHOUT
THE EMPIRE RING,
IN STITCHERY WE HERE
RECORD
THE CROWNING OF OUR
SOVEREIGN LORD.
GVIR
IN CAMP THE YOUTHS
OF BRITAIN FIND
THE HUMAN TOUCH,
THE KINGLY MIND.
E
IN HIS OWN REALM HE FOUND HIS BRIDE,
BELOVED QUEEN, HER COUNTRY'S PRIDE.
EACH DAUGHTER, IN HER SMILING FACE,
SHOWS CHILDHOOD'S MOST ENDEARING
GRACE.
NEVER, SINCE THE WORLD BEGAN,
CAME GREATER HERITAGE TO MAN.
EMPIRE AND THE MOTHERLAND
IN COMMON CAUSE TOGETHER STAND.
PEACE FROM THE CARES OF STATE,
ONCE THROUGH THE GARDEN GATE.
GOOD HEALTH
UNTO THEIR MAJESTIES
WITH HONOUR, HAPPINESS, AND PEACE.
UNCOUNTED LOYAL SUBJECTS SING
LONG MAY HE REIGN-
GOD SAVE THE KING.

1987-1997

Social history made more appealing.

By demonstrating changes over time from 1805 to the present, St Fagans: National History Museum makes the history of a terraced row of homes remarkably accessible. The Rhyd-y-car houses, opened in 1988, display a past that we can identify with, and show that culture is not static.

Left and above: A tapestry hung in one of the Rhyd-y-car houses.

Part of a terrace originally built around 1800, these houses now reflect the history of the ordinary people of Merthyr Tydfil over two centuries. Each house represents a different period, demonstrating changes in buildings, gardens, furniture, furnishings and living conditions. Much is based on the memories of former occupants.

1805 The majority of occupants at Rhyd-y-car work at a nearby iron-ore pit. In this house, a young couple from west Wales have brought the oak furniture given to them as wedding presents, as is usual at this time. The windows don't open and there are no toilets – the occupants use the nearby canal and cinder tips. There is a pigsty at the bottom of the garden.

1855 Neither ventilation nor sanitation have improved. This house is occupied by forty-eight-year-old widow Margaret Rosser and her children. She earns her living as a milkwoman – Mr Rosser, an ironstone miner, died four years ago. Her nineteen-year-old son is a coal miner, part of Merthyr's new prime industry.

1895 The Rhyd-y-car houses are surrounded by rail and tram lines. The inhabitant of this house is William Richards, a railway signalman originally from Pembrokeshire. He lives here with his wife and daughter. Their house has sash windows and an outside toilet, which they share with the neighbours. The interior is decorated with pictures, souvenirs and brass knick-knacks.

1925 These houses are now considered very small and old fashioned. To make the best use of the single downstairs living room, one half – known as the 'best side' and always facing the door – is furnished with better-quality furniture than the rest of the house. Water has been introduced to the house and the main room has been wallpapered.

1955 This house has a kitchenette. The marital bedroom has been moved upstairs, with a small bedroom for a child taking its place. A shed in the garden opposite the front door serves as an extra living area, allowing the house to be kept for best.

1985 Although most of the Rhyd-y-car houses were demolished, similar terraces survive. This house shows how such dwellings were adapted to meet the needs of life in the late twentieth century. For the first time, the house and its contents represent a clear break with the past – this house could be anywhere in Britain.

The history of a working Welsh community.

Wales's iron industry employed both men and women in large numbers. In 1850, more than 600 women worked for the ironworks of Merthyr Tydfil. Pollers would load ore from the trams and pile it up for the furnaces, ironstone girls broke up large lumps of iron ore, coke girls stacked coking coal, brickyard girls helped clear the trams and pilers weighed the iron. Until 1842, women and children worked underground.

At the end of the nineteenth century, Merthyr Tydfil was one of Britain's most heavily industrialised areas. This can be traced back to the fact that the eighteenth century saw many great English ironmasters arrive there to make use of the ironstone that occurred naturally in the area.

Among these was Richard Crawshay, who opened the Cyfarthfa ironworks in 1765. Around 1800, Crawshay built the Rhyd-y-car terrace for his ironworkers. The houses were all of a particular type associated with the Crawshays, having two storeys, with a single room on each floor measuring 4m x 3.8m. A small single-storey extension at the back contained the main bedroom and a small pantry.

Nearly 400 such houses were built in the south Wales valleys. The Rhyd-y-car houses were the smallest and represented the minimum standard acceptable to the Crawshay family. In 1851, as many as 169 people lived in the 29 houses.

Above and right: The Rhyd-y-car ironworkers' houses as re-erected at St Fagans.

Inadequate sanitation led to cholera, which struck Merthyr Tydfil in 1849 and 1854. Rhyd-y-car suffered six deaths. As a result, fixed windows were replaced with opening sash or casement windows, piped water was provided to standpipes and the first drainage system was installed. Three communal ovens were also built.

By 1881, there were no ironworkers living at Rhyd-y-car. The main employer now, and until the 1960s, was coal mining. Ten years later, the houses were considered out-dated and cramped. However, number 14 Rhyd-y-car still had ten occupants.

The worldwide economic slump of 1926 hit Merthyr hard. Between 1921 and 1931 a massive 12,000 jobs were lost. Around 17,000 people left the area. During this time, most of the Rhyd-y-car houses were sold by the Crawshay family.

The houses were condemned in the mid-1930s and, in December 1979, a flood finally sealed their fate. In 1986, the Museum was given six of the houses from Merthyr Tydfil Borough Council. The rest were demolished.

The past is brought to life – brick by brick.

The re-erection and refurbishment of the Rhyd-y-car houses broke new ground in the world of open-air museums. For the first time, visitors were able to view not simply a period interior, but also how that interior had changed over the course of nearly two hundred years.

Since St Fagans opened as a museum in 1948, more than forty buildings from all parts of Wales have been relocated to the expansive site. They depict the lives of the people of Wales from the Middle Ages to the present day. The collection comprises a variety of building types, including farmhouses, agricultural outbuildings, mills, dwellings, craft workshops, commercial premises, a school, a workmen's institute and places of worship.

Buildings are only accepted for removal to the Museum if they are threatened with demolition or collapse. Dismantling them and giving them a new home at St Fagans ensures their future and preserves a link with the past.

Staff from the Museum's specialist Historic Buildings Unit are responsible for the study, collection, re-erection and maintenance of the buildings. In each case, they painstakingly record and dismantle the buildings, carefully numbering each important piece of masonry and timber. The materials are then transported to St Fagans where they are reassembled like a giant 3D jigsaw. Staff use traditional tools, materials and techniques appropriate to the period the building was originally constructed.

The Museum's mission is to bring history to life. While the Historic Buildings Unit re-erects the buildings, other departments help to recreate the interiors. Curatorial staff carry out extensive research into the people, tools, ornaments and furnishings connected with the buildings. This can sometimes take years. In the case of Rhyd-y-car, curators were able to interview former occupants and to turn the houses into real people's homes. Attention to detail is important, even down to a bowler hat seen in the 1925 house.

Left and above: The work of re-erecting the Rhyd-y-car houses.

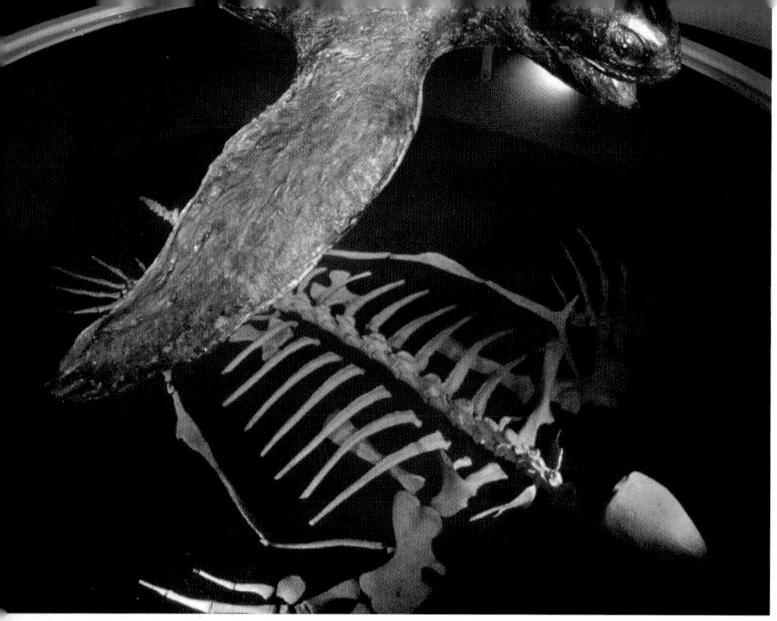

A record-breaking friend from the deep drops in.

The largest leatherback turtle ever recorded was stranded on the beach below Harlech Castle in September 1988. Its valuable legacy was to help us develop a better understanding of its incredibly varied natural habitats.

The year 1988 was a vintage year for watchers of leatherback turtles around Britain. A total of thirty such fabulous deep-sea visitors were spotted off the coast between June and October. It's possible they had been attracted by that year's exceptional numbers of jellyfish – their staple diet – drifting with the Gulf Stream in the southwestern approaches of Britain and Ireland.

They had travelled a long way. Those seen off the British Isles are thought to come from the Caribbean or northern South America. They once bred in the Mediterranean, but are now extinct there, and leatherbacks are listed as an endangered species.

Nine leatherbacks were found dead on Britain's beaches in 1988, four of them in Wales. One of these, a fine male specimen, was taken to the Museum. It was put quickly into cold store at –10°C to preserve its tissues, and was soon discovered to be the largest and heaviest recorded, winning it a place in the *Guinness Book of Records*. It was 291cm long, 277cm from flipper tip to flipper tip and weighed 916kg.

The turtle was studied carefully while being prepared for display. A special feature of leatherback turtles is their fat, which is thought to help them regulate their body temperature. However, it also makes them particularly challenging to display. A cast was therefore taken of the Harlech turtle, and can now be seen in its own dedicated display at National Museum Cardiff.

Leatherbacks are so called because of their unique shell, which is composed of a layer of tough, rubbery skin strengthened by thousands of tiny bony plates that makes it look 'leathery'. It's the only sea turtle that lacks a hard shell and is unique among reptiles in being able to maintain its body temperature independently of surrounding environmental temperatures. This means it can both exist in temperate areas and to dive to an incredible 1,600 metres, where the cold and the pressure are intense.

Above and right: The world's largest known leatherback turtle.

rwban Môr Mwyaf y Byc
e World's Largest Turtl

An amazing journey through time is launched.

The tiny piece of the Earth that we call Wales is over 700 million years old. Throughout that time, it has drifted across the globe through many different environments and climates.

In 1993, the Museum opened *The Evolution of Wales*, the largest single exhibition ever built by the Museum, occupying over a thousand square metres of floor space. It tells the story of the evolution of Wales from its earliest geological origins up to the end of the last Ice Age, when our modern landscape was moulded.

An introductory gallery shows the processes that have shaped our planet – water, wind, ice, gravity and heat from the interior of the Earth. The evidence for these changes is locked up in the rocks, minerals and fossils beneath our feet.

The land that is now Wales has drifted slowly across the face of the Earth, from far south of the equator to its present location. The spectacular environments encountered in this fascinating journey include volcanoes, glaciers, coral reefs, tropical swamps and deserts. Dinosaurs and mammoths were just some of the animals living in these dramatic landscapes at different times.

The specimens and models in the exhibition range from tiny fossil sea-shells and corals to dinosaurs and large sea-reptiles. Films illustrate geological processes as well as modern environments worldwide that still illustrate the landscapes of millions of years ago.

The final gallery in the exhibition includes a spectacular range of animals, plants, fossils and minerals that demonstrate the diversity of the natural world – and remind us that our world is constantly changing.

Left and above: Reconstructions of *Plateosaurus* and *Hypsilophodon*, part of the exhibition *Evolution of Wales*.

Even the wild Welsh weather couldn't stop an Impressionist painter gaining great inspiration.

In 1897, Alfred Sisley (1839-1899) left France for a British trip that included six weeks in south Wales. The result was some wonderful art.

Cliff at Penarth, Evening, Low Tide shows a high cliff walk, looking southwards, with the island of Steep Holm to the left. It is an evening view, and the light rakes sharply from the west, casting purple shadows from the steep cliff over the beach below. Sisley noted his practical difficulties while working on this work when he wrote of painting 'against the wind, which reigns supreme here. I had not experienced this before.'

Sisley, the only Impressionist painter to have visited Wales, was born of English parents but lived in France. Although overshadowed in his lifetime by Monet and Renoir, Sisley remains a quintessential representative of the Impressionist movement. Heavily influenced by Turner, he concentrated on landscape subjects more than any other Impressionists.

He was invited to Britain by friend and patron François Depeaux. He and his long-term partner Eugénie Lescouezec stayed in London, Cornwall then Wales, where they married in Cardiff then honeymooned in the Gower. He was fascinated with the unique geological structure of the cliffs and the spectacular tidal fall of the Bristol Channel.

Depeaux was a collector of Impressionist work and had business dealings in Swansea and Cardiff. It was he who probably persuaded Sisley of the attractions of the Bristol Channel and the sea off Gower. This painting formerly belonged to Depeaux's brother-in-law. The Museum bought the painting with help from the Art Fund at auction in 1993.

Left: *Cliff at Penarth, Evening, Low Tide* (1897) by Alfred Sisley.

Beautiful, limited edition books produced in Wales – thanks to two dynamic sisters.

As Britain tried to pick itself up from the horrors of the First World War, a forward-thinking enterprise in mid-Wales brought joy with a mixture of traditional skills. In the 1920s Britain headed for the Great Depression. Unemployment soared, and many communities, particularly in the northern industrial towns, were shattered. There were, however, glimmers of hope – including one in the village of Tregynon, near Newtown.

For here was Gregynog Hall, the imposing home of sisters Gwendoline and Margaret Davies and where, in 1922, they established the Gregynog Press. During the next eighteen years the Press would gain a reputation for producing some of Britain's finest limited edition books. It came to be ranked alongside the leading private presses of the era.

The Press used traditional methods of printing and hand binding, carried out by time-served craftsmen. Illustrations were created by leading artists, printing was carried out on handmade papers and the finest binding materials were used.

One of their publications – *The Fables of Esope* – is now recognized as one of the finest of all private press books. It was illustrated by Agnes Miller Parker, one of the leading women in wood engraving. Parker and her husband William McCance worked at Gregynog Press from 1930 to 1933 alongside the other husband and wife team of Blair Hughes-Stanton and Gertrude Hermes. They were some of Britain's most technically brilliant and imaginative wood engravers.

The press produced forty-two titles in all, and three for private circulation. Around fifteen copies of each title would be specially bound. The special bindings, from George Fisher's in-house bindery, have been internationally acclaimed. Numerous pamphlets were also produced, including the Gregynog Music Festival programmes.

However, the social and economic climate of the 1930s finally caught up with the enterprise, and was the major contributory factor in the demise of the Gregynog Press in 1940 – and of other private presses.

The Gregynog Press was revived by the University of Wales in the 1970s. Using the traditional craftsmanship for which it is famous, Gwasg Gregynog as it is now known printed the inaugural document for the 1999 opening of the National Assembly for Wales – the first instrument of Welsh government for more than 600 years.

In 1994, Gwendoline Davies's personal collection of the Press's books, all in special bindings, were loaned to the Museum, thanks to the Gwendoline & Margaret Davies Charity.

Right: *The Fables of Esope*, published by the Gregynog Press in 1931. This is the special binding by George Fisher, designed by William McCance.

THE
FABLES
OF
ESOPE
CAXTON
THE
FABLES
OF
CAXTON

A great musical instrument dating back more than two centuries is acquired.

Sir Watkin Williams-Wynn (1749-1789) was perhaps the greatest patron of the arts Wales has ever produced. He was a patron of architects, designers and gardeners, loved the theatre and painted watercolours, tutored by Paul Sandby, a founding member of the Royal Academy. His passion for music is illustrated by this wonderful chamber organ.

The principal home of Sir Watkin Williams-Wynn was Wynnstay, near Wrexham. He inherited his estate – more than 100,000 acres in north Wales and Shropshire – at the age of six. When he came of age he gained control of an income of approximately £27,000.

He became the financial and social equal of most English peers, got to know most leading patrons of the arts and himself became the foremost private art collector in Wales. Included in his vast collection was a portrait of Welsh painter Richard Wilson by Rome-based Anton Raphael Mengs. He gave Wilson a lucrative commission worth nearly £600 and commissioned five major paintings from portrait specialist Sir Joshua Reynolds.

He was also a leading musical amateur of his time, singing, and playing the cello, harpsichord and harp. He had his own organist and harpist and gave frequent music parties.

From 1772 to 1775 Sir Watkin spent much time in London, where he employed neo-classical architect Robert Adam to build him a house in St James Square. Adam's reputation was based on his skill in co-ordinating all aspects of a building, and for his wealthy, enthusiastic Welsh patron he designed mirrors, carpets, furniture and even the table silver. The largest piece of Adam furniture from the house is the neo-classical case designed for the beautiful chamber organ crafted by great organ builder John Snetzler.

The organ was made for Sir Watkin's London home in 1774. It was altered by Samuel Green in 1783 and moved to Wynnstay Hall in 1863, rebuilt by Gray & Davison. The organ was bought by the Museum in 1995, with the help of the Art Fund and the National Heritage Memorial Fund, and arrived there in 1996 following conservation work. It is still in playing order, and is often used at the Museum for organ recitals.

Left and above: Sir Watkin Williams-Wynn's chamber organ. Right: Sir Watkin Williams-Wynn sketching by Paul Sandby.

A collaborative research and education programme is undertaken in the Indian Ocean.

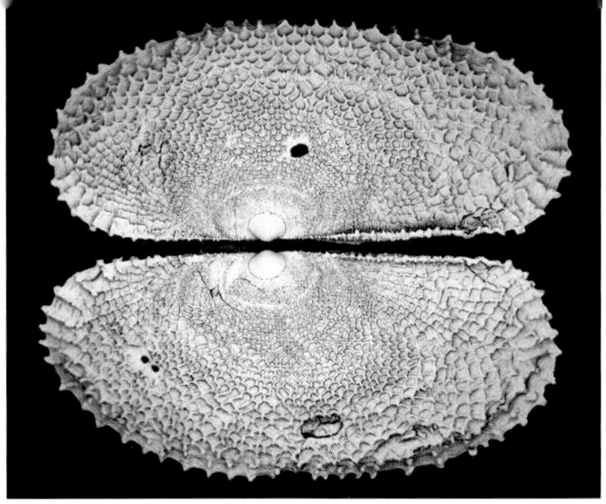

'The requirement for the conservation of our oceans transcends political boundaries. The countries of the world are therefore dependent on one another to ensure a healthy marine environment'.
Nelson Mandela

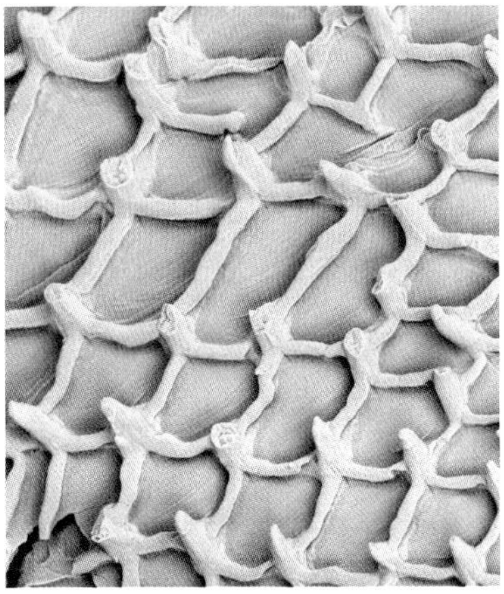

Rodrigues is a tiny tropical island, 600 km east of Mauritius, surrounded by the Indian Ocean's largest coral-fringed lagoon. It is part of the Mascarene Plateau, a spectacular submerged volcanic plateau dominating the western ocean, one of the few submerged features clearly visible from space.

Once home to the solitaire bird – a relative of the dodo – the island lost most of its forest and indigenous land fauna with human colonization, but the lagoon remained relatively unspoilt and became the major source of food for the growing human population.

Reliance on the lagoon remains, but erosion, over-fishing, population growth and tourism now threaten its health. To assess these impacts, in 1997 – the International Year of the Reef – the Royal Geographical Society, at the invitation of the governments of Mauritius and Seychelles, launched the Shoals of Capricorn Programme. However, they were hampered by the lack of identification guides to the lagoon's fauna and flora.

To address this, an international workshop of forty participants was organised in conjunction with the Museum's Department of Biodiversity and Systematic Biology.

International experts from eight countries, including Wales, were joined by delegates from the Indian Ocean region. Through the workshop, more than 1,000 species were recognized, including around 100 potentially new to science.

The results will contribute enormously to the understanding of local biodiversity and will be invaluable to future biological and ecological studies of the lagoon and reef. Between the Museum and the university colleges of Wales, Wales is in an excellent position to play a role in capacity-building in the developing world and, in doing so, increasing Wales's reputation as a centre of excellence for marine biological research.

Left: The 'Victor Cockle'
Ctenocardia victor.
Above: Detail of the bivalve shell
Galeomma sagenata.
Right: *Galeomma sagenata,* found in the Rodrigues lagoon, was new to science.

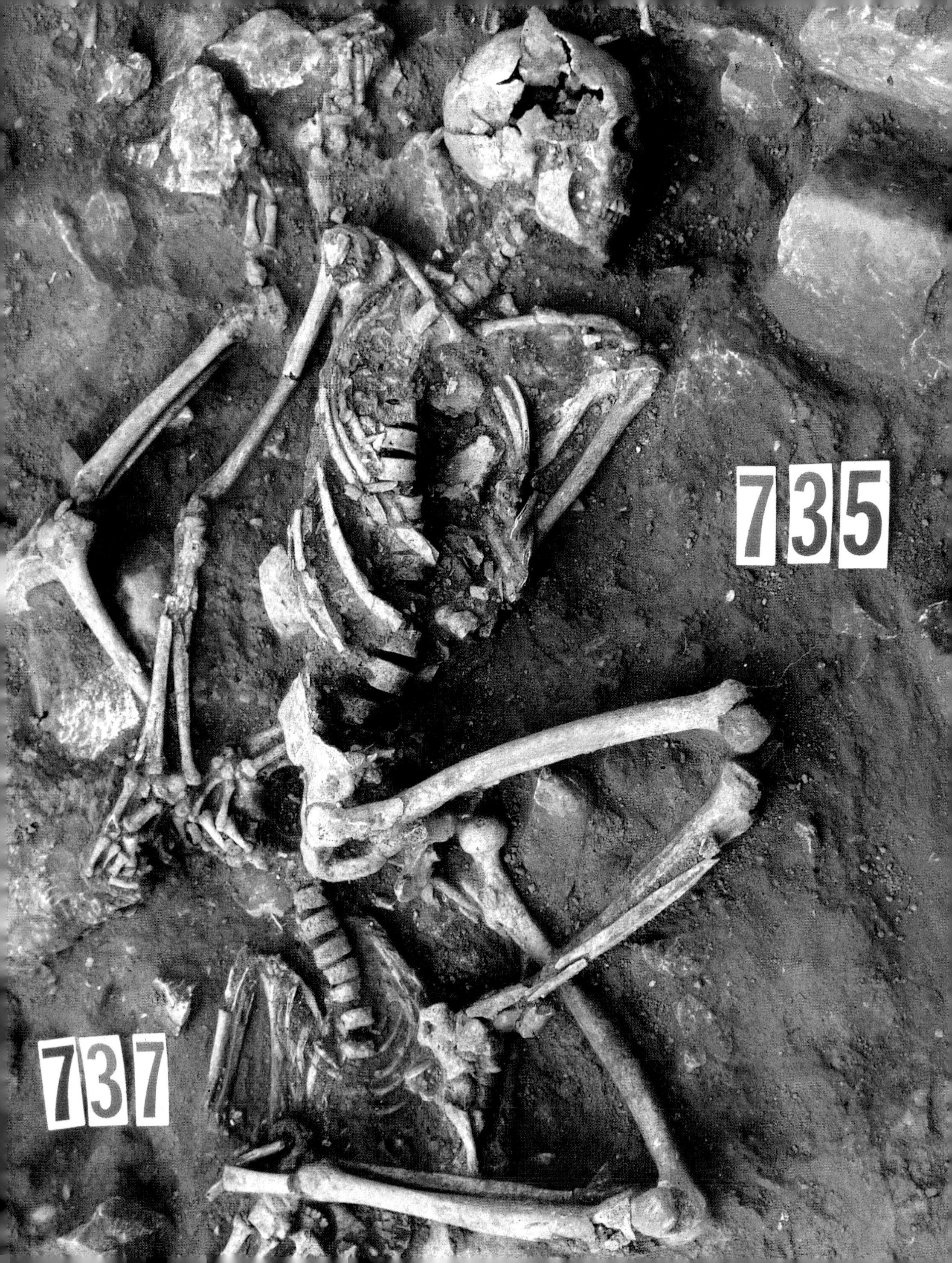
735
737

1997 - 2007

Vikings in Wales: new evidence.

Excavations of an early medieval settlement at Llanbedrgoch on the Isle of Anglesey have started to unlock details of life in ninth-tenth century Wales and the development of a Viking-age centre with trading links across the Irish Sea.

Evidence for a Viking-age settlement at Llanbedrgoch came to light between 1989 and 1992, when ninth–century coins from Kent and Carolingian France and three lead weights of Viking type were discovered by two metal detectorists.

Following these discoveries, the museum launched eight seasons of excavation on the site in 1994, to place them in their archaeological and historical contexts. Just as the excavations at Dinas Powys between 1954 and 1958 heralded a period of optimism in the archaeology of early medieval Wales up to the 800s, the excavations at Llanbedrgoch now provide a wealth of information on Viking-age Wales. The site is a Welsh counterpart to the rich Viking-age settlements in Ireland. In particular, it is illuminating the relationship between native Welsh and Vikings.

During the eighth century, the enclosed site had timber buildings and at least one large hall. In the late ninth century, the boundary was rebuilt as a massive defensive stone wall. By the twelfth century, the area then appears to have reverted to agriculture, which in time removed all surface traces of the former settlement.

In 1998-1999, a disturbing discovery was made. Five human skeletons were found in a ditch immediately outside the defensive wall. One adult male's arms appeared to have been tied behind his back, and he may have suffered a blow to the left eye with a sharp object. Another adult male may have had his wrists fastened in front of his body. We can only speculate as to the precise circumstances of their deaths, but they appear to be victims of the Vikings' search for wealth, perhaps as hostages or slaves.

What is certain is that these discoveries are changing the perception of Viking-age Wales.

Left: The skeletons of an adult male and an adolescent.
Above: Facial reconstructions of four of the people buried at Llanbedrgoch. The two on the left are from the skeletons illustrated.

A discovery centre opens for inquisitive museum visitors – and proves to be an enormous success.

Glanely Discovery Gallery at National Museum Cardiff invites visitors to get to grips with some of the 4.7 million items normally buried away in the Museum stores. The hands-on space is an interactive attraction for all ages.

Right from the Gallery's launch in 1999 it was common to find a five-year-old studying an insect through a video microscope sitting next to an adult reading up on Swansea pottery or getting the feel for marine molluscs or stone axes.

Meanwhile, a varied programme of hands-on activities became a key feature of weekends and holidays at Glanely Discovery Gallery. They still ensure a steady stream of visitors.

Unlike many drop-in sessions, Glanely's workshops can be booked up to two weeks in advance – and some have been full within half an hour of booking opening. Sessions have included Japanese kite making, fossil chipping, reptile handling (complete with large snakes!), portrait painting, felt making and archaeological reconstructions. Families can work together on projects like Mining for Chocolate or Making Nature Diaries.

Sessions are also available for schools, home-educators and special interest groups and the Gallery runs a varied series of events linked to National Museum Cardiff's exhibitions and activities.

Specialist staff are often on-hand, and Glanely facilitators are always available to arrange for plenty of creative inspiration and help with enquiries.

Right: A sample of coral, one of the many specimens that can be explored up close at Glanely Discovery Gallery.

BREAD

A row of houses reflects three crucial periods in the history of Welsh slate quarrying.

The Museum has great experience of moving and re-erecting historic buildings – as illustrated at St Fagans. So, when 1-4 Fron Haul, a row of four slateworkers' houses, was condemned in the late 1990s the Museum was quick to act. The houses, which first appear in the 1861 Census, typified the cramped terrace homes of the quarrying communities. Between 1831 and 1881 the population of boom-time Ffestiniog grew from 1,648 to 11,274, as people flooded into the slate quarrying areas to work.

In 1998 work began on moving the houses from Tanygrisiau near Blaenau Ffestiniog to the National Slate Museum in Llanberis. All the bricks and stones were individually numbered and transported and the houses were reconstructed exactly as they had been. A Heritage Lottery Fund grant ensured that 1-4 Fron Haul opened in its new home in July 1999. Three houses now reflect separate periods of slate industry history, and a fourth is an education centre.

Tanygrisiau, 1861

It's the golden age of slate, and the industry is rapidly becoming one of the most important in Wales. It's the main employer in Gwynedd. Housing cannot keep up with the explosion in work and two families often share one house. The inhabitants of this house are a married couple, the husband's brother and a lodger.

Bethesda, 1901

November last year saw 2,800 quarrymen walk out for what would become one of British industrial history's worst disputes - the Penrhyn Strike. In total, it lasted three years. In June 1901, 55 men went back to work, and feelings are strong. A card in the window reads *Nid oes Bradwr yn y tŷ hwn* – 'no traitor in this house'. The occupants are a quarryman who is on strike, his wife and three children. They depend on the 17-year-old daughter's wages, who is in service, to make ends meet.

Llanberis, 1969

The bright fashions of the day are seen in the kitchen, lighting, colourful furnishings, clothes and the 45rpm pop music singles. However, in an area where unemployment runs high, the man of the house has just been told that he is out of a job – the quarry is closing down.

Left: One of the houses represents a household from Bethesda in 1901.
Above: The terrace of houses from Fron Haul.

A homely example of post-war innovation is preserved as a reminder of the 'make do and mend' era.

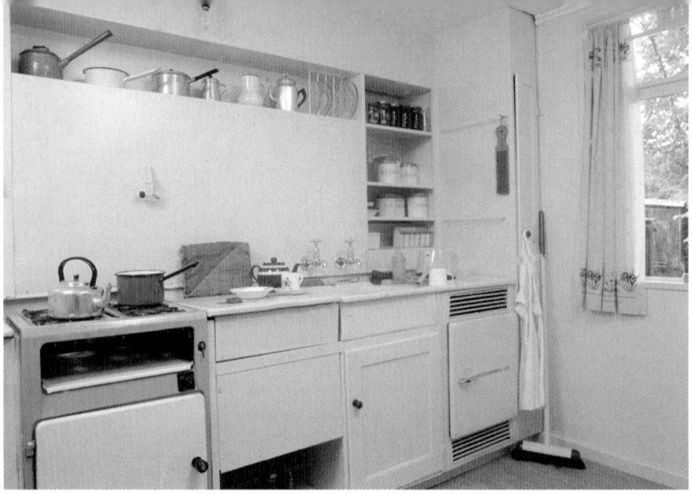

Buildings like the prefab bungalow at St Fagans were crucial to getting families from battle-scarred Britain back on their feet after the Second World War.

Britain and the Allies may have won the War, but victory came at an enormous price. Thousands of people were left homeless and this necessitated some quick thinking and a few quick fixes.

The solution included amazing aluminium prefabricated houses, that were a triumph in space planning. They were made in factories that had once produced aircraft and they flew off the production lines at the rate of one every twelve minutes.

Four versions of these 'tin palaces', as they became known, were produced, each with a similar layout. All had two bedrooms, a living room, hallway, kitchen and bathroom. They had innovative fixtures and fittings, including built-in refrigerators, fitted kitchens and warm-air heating for the bedrooms.

The prefab at St Fagans is a type B2. It comprises four sections, which were pre-assembled with all wiring, plumbing and gas pipes in place. It was reassembled at St Fagans in 2001, after being transported from Gabalfa in Cardiff, where it had been put up in 1947-8.

It is furnished as it would have appeared in 1950 and includes pieces of the now famous Utility furniture. This was a basic range of furniture produced in Britain during and after the War, made mainly of plywood due to the scarcity of timber. Those eligible were given coupons or 'units' and could order the furniture through a standard catalogue. This was also the age of 'making do', and some pieces of furniture in the St Fagans prefab would have been hand-me-downs or bought second hand.

Above and right: The prefab at St Fagans today.

Big Pit today is an award-winning national museum, but it still retains many traits of its former role as a real coal mine.

Standing high on the heather-clad moors of Blaenafon, Big Pit was incorporated into Amgueddfa Cymru – National Museum Wales on 1 February 2001. Tunnels and buildings that once echoed to the echo to the sound of the miners now enjoy the sound of the footsteps and chatter of visitors from all over the world.

Bit Pit is a living, breathing reminder of the coal industry in Wales and the people and society it created.

One of its best-known features is the world-famous underground tour. With a former miner as a guide, and kitted out in helmet and cap lamp, visitors can travel down the 90-metre (300 feet) shaft to explore underground workings dating back to the early nineteenth century.

This authentic experience is complemented by innovative galleries and displays in the colliery buildings. They feature the sights and sounds of a colliery at work and show the human face of an industry and society that helped shape the modern world.

In 2005, following a £7.1m redevelopment, Big Pit won the prestigious £100,000 Gulbenkian Prize for British Museum of the Year.

Big Pit is set in the unique industrial landscape of Blaenafon, which was designated a World Heritage Site by UNESCO in 2000 in recognition of its international importance to the process of industrialization through iron and coal production.

Above: Visitors touring at Big Pit. Right: The winding gear at Big Pit today.

Above and right: Mining images from Amgueddfa Cymru – National Museum Wales's extensive archive.

One of the South Wales Coalfield's most famous former pits is welcomed into the Museum.

Big Pit provided coal for the world and employment for the Blaenafon area for well over a century. It got its name, incidentally, from the width of its elliptical shaft. At 5.5m at its widest point, it was the first in the Blaenafon area wide enough to wind two coal drams side by side in the cage.

Big Pit is an amalgamation of several separate mines. The present shaft was sunk around 1860 although it wasn't known as Big Pit until around 1880, when it was deepened to 89m. By 1896, 528 men were employed, and by 1935 the workforce had rocketed to 2,200 men producing 600,000 tons of coal a year.

Eleven seams were worked during Big Pit's life, producing the first-class steam, house and gas coals for which south Wales was world famous.

In time, the seams became worked out or uneconomical and were closed down. The lowest seam, the Garw, was the last one to be worked. It contained top-grade coking coal, but with a maximum thickness of 750cm it became very difficult to work.

The pit was among the first in south Wales to be electrified, and by 1910 the ventilating fan, pumps and underground haulage system were all worked by electricity. However, the winding gear was driven by steam until 1953. Coal continued to be cut and and loaded by hand until well into the twentieth century.

Until 1939 miners at Big Pit travelled to and from work in their working clothes, but in that year the pithead baths opened. The miners' lockers and showers can still be seen in the pithead baths exhibition.

Welsh coal output peaked in 1913. However, slow decline followed the industrial recession in the 1920s, and Blaenafon saw 57% unemployment. Work picked up during the Second World War as coal became a vital commodity, but peace brought reduced demand, and by 1966 Big Pit was the only deep mine left in the Blaenafon area. When the mine closed in 1980, the workforce had fallen to 227. In April 1983 Big Pit reopened as a visitor attraction, and in 2001 was incorporated into the Museum.

Visitor numbers shoot up as entry to the Museum becomes free.

The late 1990s saw a UK Government commitment to reinstate free entry at national museums. The pledge followed a lengthy debate on the matter – and the result would prove very popular.

April 2001 was a milestone in the life of the Museum. It was the month when the Welsh Assembly Government introduced free entry – several months before it was introduced in England. The Museum saw an amazing increase of 88% in visitor figures – a staggering 1.4 million visitors. This increase far exceeded any other national museum outside London.

Free entry for all followed the Museum's April 1999 decision to allow free admittance for school parties. At some museums, the 2001 move was almost overwhelming. St Fagans experienced a 116% increase in visits, while the National Slate Museum saw a staggering 168% rise.

Right: The Main Hall at National Museum Cardiff.

Discovered! One of the finest Roman vessels found in Wales.

In November 2002, a metal detectorist discovered a small, upturned vessel lying next to the figure of a crouching animal in a pit. The beautifully crafted leopard had originally formed the handle of the vessel. Investigation revealed that that the vessel had been buried with the remains of a cremation close to a Roman road and not far from the Roman fort at Abergavenny (Gobannium).

Above and Right: This Roman leopard cup, found on a farm near Abergavenny, was probably a drinking vessel.

The Romans completed the occupation of south Wales in AD 74-75. It is unknown whether the vessel belonged to a member of the Roman army or a native Briton. Whoever the owner was, this finely decorated vessel – manufactured with impressive craftsmanship in the first century AD and buried with its owner – must have been a highly prized possession.

The finder reported the object promptly to the Portable Antiquities Scheme, which enabled an archaeological investigation of the place of discovery. Sensibly, he did not to try to clean the cup, but took it to a museum as he had discovered it. This avoided further damage and allowed researchers to gain as much information as possible.

The leopard is such an accurate and naturalistic model that it was probably produced by someone with first-hand knowledge of big cats. The vessel was almost certainly made in Italy, where such animals were imported in the Early Empire. In Roman mythology, the leopard is a companion of Bacchus, the god of wine, so the vessel was probably used as a drinking cup or small jug.

Both vessel and leopard handle are made from leaded bronze, and detailed conservation work and scientific analysis have revealed that the leopard's spots are silver and its eyes were inlaid with amber. The face has been depicted in very fine detail, with minutely cast canine teeth and incised lines for its whiskers. The marks where the paws had been soldered to the vessel were still visible, and the whole cup was so finely crafted that the handle could be exactly reattached in its original position.

A new way of understanding those chance archaeological discoveries.

A series of high-profile Welsh finds by members of the public has demonstrated the success of a forward-thinking initiative to create a greater understanding of our past.

The Portable Antiquities Scheme encourages the voluntary reporting of archaeological objects found by members of the public. Many items legally defined as Treasure first come to light through the Scheme.

The Scheme promotes public awareness of the importance of such finds for understanding our past. Since 1997, more than 200,000 objects have been recorded in England and Wales. Many important discoveries have been reported in Wales – for instance, the spectacular Abergavenny leopard cup and the Limoges cross.

The cross came to light when a member of the public reported a large collection of objects which had been found before the Scheme had been introduced. Within the collection were some important enamelled copper alloy Romanesque plaques and gilt mounts. They appear to be derived from a single altar cross, produced in the Limoges area of central France. The T-shaped plaques depict the Evangelists, the central plaque depicts Christ and the gilt mounts depict John the Baptist and Mary. Important contextual information, now lost, may have been retrieved had the Scheme been available when the find was discovered.

Many Welsh finds are now being reported thanks to a good relationship with the metal detecting community, but there are other productive finders, such as field walkers. A forestry worker reported significant scatters of Stone Age flint tools from the upland areas of Glamorgan, where previously we had little knowledge of any activity. For this, Phil Shepherd received the Tarmac Finders Award presented at the British Archaeological Awards in 2000 and an MBE in 2005 for services to forestry and archaeology. Other flint collectors are busy in Pembrokeshire and Gower, producing evidence of extensive Stone Age activity. Another highlight of the Scheme has been large collections of Bronze Age metalwork reported by metal detector users, which have provided archaeologists with fascinating new insights into this important period in Wales's past.

The Scheme is managed in Wales by the Museum and is operated with the help of the Welsh Archaeological Trusts and local museums.

Left: Detail of the central medallion depicting Christ. Above: Twelfth-century enamelled plaques and mounts from an altar cross before conservation.

Cutting-edge technology throws new light on traditional industries.

Visitors to the National Waterfront Museum can wallow in wealth, dabble with danger and risk their health. They can even be plunged into poverty.
It's a new spin on the old favourite of spending a few hours immersed in history.

Cutting-edge technology now brings Wales's industrial heritage to life – through words, pictures, films, maps, spoken testimony and the latest sensory technology.

Among the innovative approaches at the National Waterfront Museum are projections that respond to gestures. Tabletops with sensors mean that visitors can interact with the displays. Traditional exhibition methods are used in new ways: three huge upright moving loops show changing displays, and as each display case descends to visitor level it triggers the appropriate information on an adjoining screen.

Much effort has been put into providing physical and cultural access. Words are both spoken and written, and it is one of the first museums in the UK to feature multilingual voiceovers as well as sign language.

The Museum is housed in a magnificent building that elegantly combines old and new architecture. A Grade II listed former dockside warehouse (formerly the Swansea Maritime & Industrial Museum) built in 1901 is contrasted with a spectacular new glass and slate structure.

Opened in 2005, it represents one of Amgueddfa Cymru – National Museum Wales's biggest, most ambitious projects. It was developed in partnership with the City & County of Swansea and was made possible by an £11million Heritage Lottery Fund grant.

It has already scooped a Regeneration Award for the best design-led regeneration project in the UK, and an award from the Royal Institute for British Architects for its architecture and design.

Above: The exterior of the National Waterfront Museum.
Right: The main foyer (top) and hi-tech senses room.

T. LETTON

POWER & INFLUENCE

A salute to the world's first industrial nation.

Wales powered the Industrial Revolution with its coal, copper, iron, steel and slate industries. Raw materials from Wales built factories and homes all over the world. The lives of Welsh people were transformed forever. So how should the Museum tell this story? Well, it's been one of the Museum's major strategic activities for the past decade.

Following redevelopment in 1998, the National Slate Museum in north Wales enjoyed a 600 per cent increase in visits and won the Wales Tourist Board's 'Sense of Place' Award 2002 for the creation of a distinctively Welsh ambience. At Big Pit in Blaenafon, redevelopment work worth £7 million was completed in 2004, and it went on to win the Gulbenkian prize for 'Museum of the Year' in 2005. The National Wool Museum in Carmarthenshire re-opened in 2004, after a £1.7 million face-lift.

The closure of the Welsh Industrial & Maritime Museum in Cardiff presented an opportunity to display the industrial collections in new and innovative ways. The culmination of the Industrial Strategy came with the opening in October 2005 of the £34 million National Waterfront Museum. The Museum was developed in partnership with the City & County of Swansea, with an £11 million grant from the Heritage Lottery Fund – the largest grant ever awarded in Wales.

A new Collections Centre was also developed, to store, care for and provide access to collections not on permanent display. Aspects of Welsh industrial life can also be found at St Fagans, with its terrace of ironworkers' houses, shops and a workmen's institute.

The combined total capital investment in the Industrial Strategy has exceeded £40 million, with significant funding provided by the Heritage Lottery Fund, the Welsh Development Agency, the Wales Tourist Board, EU funds and the Welsh Assembly Government as well as the museum itself.

Left: Road construction gang in the late nineteenth century.

Buried treasure.

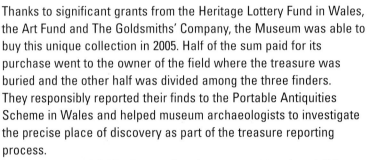

A hoard of spectacular Bronze Age gold adornments and bronze tools, buried for more than 3,000 years, was dug up by three metal detectorists near Wrexham and declared Treasure in 2004.

Thanks to significant grants from the Heritage Lottery Fund in Wales, the Art Fund and The Goldsmiths' Company, the Museum was able to buy this unique collection in 2005. Half of the sum paid for its purchase went to the owner of the field where the treasure was buried and the other half was divided among the three finders. They responsibly reported their finds to the Portable Antiquities Scheme in Wales and helped museum archaeologists to investigate the precise place of discovery as part of the treasure reporting process.

Dating to the Middle Bronze Age, between 1300 and 1150 BC, the hoard contains some fine examples of that period's goldwork. They are of international importance and demonstrate the high skills of goldworkers in Atlantic Europe at this time. Originally buried in a pottery vessel, the hoard comprises a flange-twisted torc, a wire-twisted bracelet, a necklace pendant, four beads, three rings, two palstave axes and a chisel. A fragment of the pottery vessel base also survived.

It is speculated that the hoard once belonged to a wealthy farmer of high standing or to a metal trader, either living in or travelling to this agriculturally and metal-rich region of Wales. It is a mystery as to why this spot was chosen, as there is no evidence of settlements or burial sites in the immediate vicinity. It was probably buried deliberately near the River Alyn as a votive offering to the pagan gods.

Above and right: This hoard represents some of the finest examples of Bronze Age gold.

A beautiful medieval church is re-erected in a pioneering museum project.

For the first time in Britain, a church of solid masonry construction has been moved and re-erected. St Teilo's Church was transported from Llandeilo Tal-y-bont to St Fagans, and has been painstakingly restored to its original glory using original craft techniques.

St Teilo's Church is believed to have been originally built in the thirteenth century. During the fourteenth and fifteenth centuries porch doors, north and south chapels and extra aisles were added. The oldest surviving feature is the stone font, which is thought to date from the eleventh century.

During the conservation work, a beautiful set of wall paintings were found that have been dated to the early 1500s. The whole Church has therefore been recreated as it might have appeared at this period.

The Museum's specialist Historic Buildings Unit used medieval techniques to restore the building wherever possible. During the reconstruction work, a special exhibition room was built next to the site so that visitors could find out about the the whole process.

In order to restore St Teilo's faithfully to its pre-Reformation glory, specialist artists in medieval painting techniques have been commissioned to recreate the Rood loft. Using traditional pigments and original colours they have recreated paintwork and gilding. The research for this project took many years due to the fact that no complete pre-Reformation Churches survive in Wales today.

The Church has travelled over fifty miles from its home to St Fagans open-air museum. The project is probably unique, combining art history with archaeology, building, social history and conservation, and has taken over ten years to complete.

This project is an example of valuable museum work that would not be possible without generous funding from private sources.

Above: The carved ceiling was rebuilt using traditional methods. Right: This fine pre-Reformation wall painting dates from the fifteenth century.

Current and future developments

In the run up to our centenary, we have of course been reflecting on how the Museum has developed, but, just as importantly, we have also been looking to the future. In order to meet the challenges of a national museum in the twenty-first century, we have developed a vision for the future of Amgueddfa Cymru – National Museum Wales, and that is to create a 'World Class Museum of Learning'.

By consulting widely, we have developed ideas to make visiting the national collections an even better experience, and to make the ways the collections tell their stories more meaningful to even more people.

Major plans for the future include developing the current National Museum Cardiff into a National Museum of Natural History and a National Museum of Art. We are also in ongoing discussions with the public and other national organizations on the long-term display of art in Wales. Also at National Museum Cardiff, the major exhibition *Origins* will portray the story of Wales from earliest times to the sixteenth century. This exhibition will be the first redisplay of our archaeological collections for over thirty years. It will precede moving the archaeological collections to St Fagans, as part of plans to develop that museum into a comprehensive National History Museum for Wales. As part of this development, the innovative new gallery Oriel 1 at St Fagans, which explores Welsh identities today, opened in spring 2007.

We are also developing a 'virtual museum' of Wales. This will be a website where we can publish articles, images and features about our collections. This will help us fulfil our aim to broaden access to the national collections of Wales to new audiences whoever, and wherever, they are in the world.

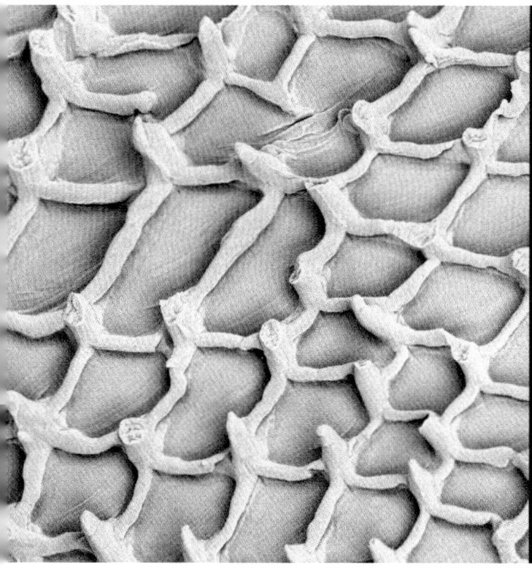

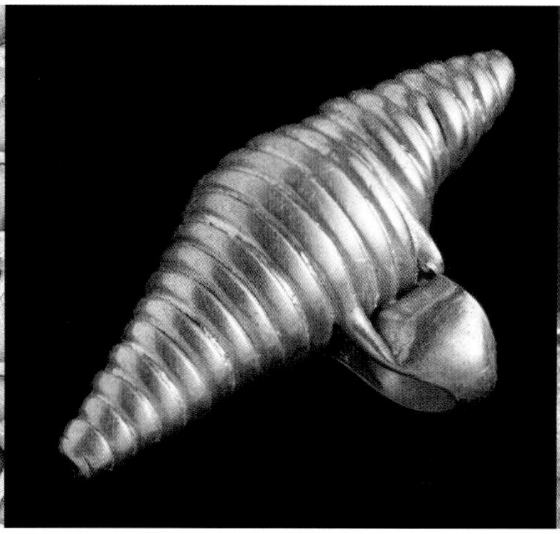

Interesting facts and figures

Amgueddfa Cymru – National Museum Wales looks after an extensive array of artefacts, historical records and cultural heritage. The Museum also has some impressive facts and figures of its own;

- The collections at Amgueddfa Cymru – National Museum Wales contain 4.7 million objects.

- Amgueddfa Cymru – National Museum Wales receives a million and a half visitors a year.

- Amgueddfa Cymru – National Museum Wales is one of the youngest national museums and galleries in the UK. Its inception dates from the 1880s when there was a movement in Wales towards the establishment of national institutions, out of which also grew the University of Wales (1893) and the National Library (1907).

- Out of the UK's network of national museums and galleries, Amgueddfa Cymru – National Museum Wales is the only one to operate as many as six museums outside the capital city or in its immediate vicinity.

- The *Which? Guide to Tourist attractions* in 2000 described Amgueddfa Cymru – National Museum Wales as one of Britain's top ten museums.

- St Fagans: National History Museum opened in 1948 and was the UK's first open-air museum. Today, St Fagans leads the field ahead of ten or so such UK museums that now exist.

- St Fagans is the most visited heritage attraction in Wales.

- Amgueddfa Cymru – National Museum Wales is the only UK museum to operate bilingually.

- Amgueddfa Cymru – National Museum Wales offers formal advice and expertise to a wide range of bodies such as the Heritage Lottery Fund, the Capital Taxes Offices, the Reviewing Committee on the Export of Works of Art, and the National Museums Directors Conference.

- The Museum's activities are funded by the Welsh Assembly Government. This is supplemented by raising its own income through grants, donations and fundraising.

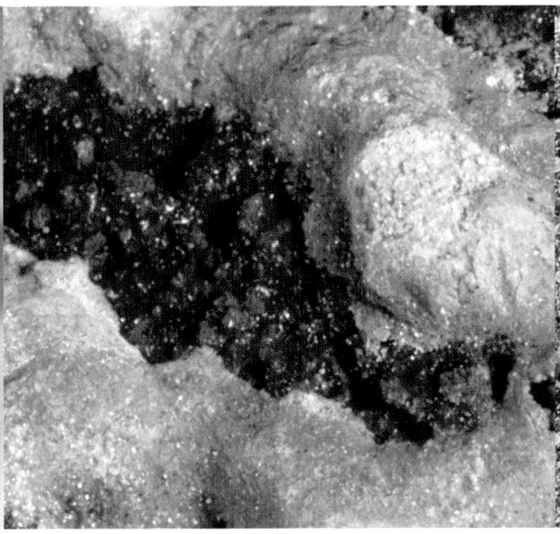

Information on the seven museums

National Museum Cardiff

Cathays Park, Cardiff CF10 3NP Wales, UK Tel: (029) 2057 3951

Although not the oldest of Amgueddfa Cymru – National Museum Wales's buildings, this is the first location of the National Museum of Wales, officially opened in 1927. It is situated in the heart of Cardiff's elegant civic centre. Today it houses Wales's national archaeology, art, geology and natural history collections.

St Fagans: National History Museum

St Fagans, Cardiff CF5 6XB Wales, UK Tel: (029) 2057 3500

St Fagans opened as the 'Welsh Folk Museum' in 1948, following the donation of the Castle and grounds by the third Earl of Plymouth. Today the 100-acre site on Cardiff's outskirts displays over forty re-erected buildings, illustrating life in all regions of Wales since Celtic times. The galleries now include the exciting and innovative Oriel 1 space, with changing exhibitions exploring life and identity in today's Wales.

Big Pit: National Coal Museum

Blaenafon, Rhondda Cynon Taf NP4 9XP Wales, UK Tel: (01495) 790311

Big Pit became part of Amgueddfa Cymru – National Museum Wales in 2000. After major redevelopment, it re-opened in 2004 and went straight on to win the prestigious Gulbenkian Prize for Museum of the Year. The redevelopment turned the original features, like the pithead baths, into fresh displays that bring life at the coalface vividly into focus. However, perhaps its most famous feature is still the trip, accompanied by an ex-miner, 90 metres under the ground.

The National Roman Legion Museum

High Street, Caerleon, Newport NP18 1AE Wales, UK
Tel: (01633) 423134

This museum was built on the site of one of only three permanent settlements built by the Romans in Britain. In 1930 it became part of Amgueddfa Cymru – National Museum Wales. Today visitors can explore a reconstruction of the centurion's barracks and the remains of the settlement including a bath house and amphitheatre. The galleries display details from Roman life that have been discovered on the site over time.

The National Slate Museum

Gilfach Goch, Llanberis, Gwynedd LL55 4TY Wales, UK
Tel: (01248) 870630

The National Slate Museum opened in 1973 in Gilfach Goch, the original quarry workshops. The workshops had once provided everything needed to run Dinorwig Quarry, which closed in 1969. Smithies, sawing sheds and a pattern loft – where moulds were handmade for any and every piece of machinery needed – have been conserved just as they were. In 1999 a row of four quarry workers' houses was re-erected on the site. The houses now illustrate three key periods in the history of the slate industry and provide a dedicated space for school visits.

The National Waterfront Museum

Oystermouth Road, Swansea, SA1 3RD Wales, UK
Tel: (01972) 638950

Amgueddfa Cymru – National Museum Wales's latest museum, located in Swansea's rapidly developing maritime quarter. The Museum was created to tell the story of the Industrial Revolution in Wales, and Wales's effect on the rest of the world during this period of transformations. The galleries include high-tech interactive displays as well as large industrial objects from the industrial and maritime collections.

The National Wool Museum

Dre-fach Felindre, Carmarthenshire, SA44 5UP Wales, UK
Tel: (01559) 370929

The National Wool Museum is on the site of Cambrian Mills, a former working woollen mill. It explores what life was like for the people who worked in Wales's wool industry, which was once on such a huge scale in west Wales that the local area was nicknamed 'the Huddersfield of Wales'. The galleries were redeveloped in 2003 and are now full of artefacts and stories straight from local life.
The Museum also houses the national flat textile collection.

www.museumwales.ac.uk

General information

Amgueddfa Cymru – National Museum Wales is a national institution, with seven museums located throughout Wales housing the Welsh national collections. Its main source of funding is the Welsh Assembly Government.

The collections are cared for by various departments. The Department of Art covers the national art and applied art collections, and is based at National Museum Cardiff. The Department of Archaeology & Numismatics covers the history of the people of Wales to the Middle Ages; the main collection is based at National Museum Cardiff but much is also displayed at the National Roman Legion Museum. The Department of Geology, based at National Museum Cardiff, covers the physical formation of Wales and how it relates to the rest of Planet Earth. The Department of Biodiversity and Systematic Biology is a combination of the former Botany and Zoology departments; it covers the huge variety of natural history and is housed at National Museum Cardiff. The Department of Industry covers the major industries of Wales. Based at the National Waterfront Museum, it encompasses the National Slate Museum, the National Wool Museum and Big Pit.

The Department of Social & Cultural History, based at St Fagans, cares for all aspects of life in Wales since the Middle Ages including sport, work, education and religion. Of course some items in our collections relate to more than one department. For example, a painting of a ship can be both a record of Wales's maritime history and a fine piece of art.

The collections could not be curated – that is, researched, explained and displayed – without being physically cared for. The Conservation Department has officers in various departments and museums, who analyse objects scientifically, often revealing new information, and either restore or preserve the object so that it can be displayed safely. Of course, some objects will always be too fragile for display, and sometimes models are made of them for display, with the original kept in special conditions. Other collections are used specifically for research purposes. Constant academic research keeps the Museum's expertise, and consequently the exhibitions and displays, at a world-class standard. When items enter the national collections, they are 'accessioned', which means they are carefully documented and possibly photographed by the Photography Unit. A standard level of information for every object is recorded. Much of this information on the 4.7 million items in the collections is now computerized, which makes it much easier to answer enquiries.

The Museum's curators deal with all sorts of enquiries. Some are from official sources, for example advice on how species are affected by changes to their environment. Most are from the public, from people seeking information on family treasures, or about objects or creatures discovered in the garden or while walking. If you have an enquiry, call the relevant museum (see the telephone number on pages 178 –179) and staff will be happy to put you in touch with an expert! The number of visitors to the museums varies from year to year. Sometimes museums have to respond to external circumstances, ranging from floods to foot and mouth disease – both of which have caused some of Wales's national museums to close temporarily. However, when free entry was introduced in 2001, thanks to support from the Welsh Assembly Government, the number of visitors rose substantially, and the year 2006/2007 saw more than 1.5 million visits – the highest number ever.

Visitors come in families, as students, tourists from the rest of Britain and abroad and school groups. They come for a day, an afternoon or a lunch hour. Any kind of group – educational, community, tourist – can arrange their visit and discuss their needs beforehand. A team of staff from the Learning Department or the Marketing Department are happy to make any necessary arrangements – call (029) 2057 3240 to speak to the Learning Department or (029) 2057 3174 to speak to the Marketing Department. The Learning Department also runs an Outreach Service, where museum objects are loaned so that they can be studied and enjoyed by schools, colleges and community groups all over Wales.

A wealth of information about Amgueddfa Cymru – National Museum Wales can be found on the website – www.museumwales.ac.uk. Information about the collections is shared with other experts in academic journals and books, and with the general public in books published by the Museum's own imprint – National Museum Wales Books. From 2007, yet more information about the collections will be available online as articles and features on a dynamic, ever-changing 'virtual museum'.

Extra funding and support for all this work, and with making new purchases to keep the collections up to date, is absolutely essential. Income is raised by the shops, cafes and by hiring out facilities and locations. Other sources range from Lottery and European Union Funding to charitable trusts, businesses and private individuals.

For more information phone the Development Department on (029) 2057 3184.

List of directors

Dr William Evans Hoyle 1908-1924

Sir Mortimer Wheeler 1925-1926

Sir Cyril F. Fox 1926-1948

Dr D. Dilwyn John 1948-1968

Dr G. O. Jones 1968-1977

Dr Douglas Bassett 1977-1985

Dr David W. Dykes 1986-1989

Alistair Wilson 1989-1993

Colin Ford 1993-1998

Anna Southall 1998-2002

Michael Houlihan 2003-

Further reading

BEVINS, R. E. 1994. *A Mineralogy of Wales.* National Museum Wales Books. ISBN 0720004039.

BREWER, R. J. 1987. *Caerleon and the Roman Army.* National Museum Wales Books. ISBN 0720004888.

BURROW, S. 2006. *The Tomb Builders in Wales 4000-3000BC.* National Museum Wales Books. ISBN 072000568X.

EDITED BY BUTLER, C. & DAVIS, M. 2006. *Things Fall Apart: Museum Conservation in Practice.* National Museum Wales Books. ISBN 0720005590.

EVANS, M. & FAIRCLOUGH, O. *A Companion Guide to the Art Galleries.* National Museum Wales Books. ISBN 0720004314.

EVANS, M. L. 1989. *The Derek Williams Collection.* National Museum Wales Books. ISBN 0720003288.

GERWYN THOMAS, W. *Big Pit Blaenavon.* National Museum Wales Books. ISBN 0720002338.

HYWEL, E. ap 2002. *Welsh Slate Museum Guide.* National Museum Wales Books. ISBN 720005132.

MORGAN, P. J. 1990. *The Leatherback Turtle: Sea Turtles and their Conservation.* National Museum Wales Books. ISBN 0720003385.

OWEN JONES, S. 1993. *The Penydarren Locomotive.* National Museum Wales Books.

REDKNAP, M. 2000. *Vikings in Wales: An Archaeological Quest.* National Museum Wales Books. ISBN 072000487X.

SHARPE, T. & MCCARTNEY, P. J. 1998. *The Papers of H. T. De la Beche (1796-1855) in the National Museum of Wales.* National Museum Wales Books. ISBN 0720004543.

SUMNER, A. 2005. *Colour and Light: Fifty Impressionist and Post-Impressionist Works at the National Museum of Wales.* National Museum Wales Books. ISBN 0720005515.

THOMAS, B. A. 1986. *In Search of Fossil Plants: the life and work of David Davies (Gilfach Goch).* National Museum Wales Books. ISBN 0720003059.

TREW, A. 1987. *James Cosmo Melvill's New Molluscan Names.* National Museum Wales Books. ISBN 0720003105.

TREW, A. 1990. *John R.le B.Tomlin's New Molluscan Names.* National Museum Wales Books. ISBN 07200 03407.

WILIAM, E. 1993. *Rhyd-y-car: A Welsh Mining Community.* National Museum Wales Books. ISBN 0720005396.

ZIENKIEWICZ, D. A. 1987. *Roman Gems from Caerleon.* National Museum Wales Books. ISBN 0720003148.

Index

A

Abergavenny 74, 162, 165
Aberllyn Mine 121
Adam, Robert 144
Andrews, Michael 126
Anning, Mary 39
Apperley, Thomas 64
Architectural competition 7
Art Fund 93, 141, 144, 170
Assheton Smith Family 104

B

Batoni, Pompeo 64
Bethesda 153
Big Pit 156, 159, 169
Blaenafon 156, 159, 169
Blaenau Ffestiniog 153
Blaker, Hugh 90
Botanical wax models 87
Böttger, Johann Friedrich 23
Brewer, Cecil Claude 7
Bronze Age 165, 170
Bryological Society 100
Burton Hoard 170
Bute, Third Marquess of 51

C

Caerleon 35, 44, 117
Caerleon Antiquarian Association 44
Cambrian Mills 123, 125
Cambrian Pottery 73
Cardiff Naturalist's Society 21, 46
Cathays Park 16, 19, 30, 36, 113
Celtic art 59
Cephalopods, Cephalopoda 12
Cézanne, Paul 70, 90
Charter 4
Christie's Auction Rooms 78
City Hall, Cardiff 16, 19, 55
Clydach Vale 32
Coins 118, 149
Conway, Charles 15
Cornforth, Fanny 26
Crawshay, Richard 132
Cronenburgh, Adriaen van 80
Crwth 43
Cryptogamic Herbarium 100

D

Darwin, Charles 24, 39
Davies Sisters 55, 90
Davies, David (fossils) 32
Davies, David (Llandinam) 90
Davies, Gwendoline 19, 55, 70, 90, 142
Davies, Margaret Sidney 19, 89, 90, 142
Davies, Sir Walford 36
De le Beche, Henry Thomas 39
De Neubourg, Henry 118
Depeaux, François 141
Derek Williams Trust 127, 129
Dinorwig Quarry 103, 104, 107
Dre-fach Felindre 123, 125
Duke of Beaufort 93
Dunbar Smith, Arnold 7

E

Earl of Plymouth 60, 63, 66
Elizabeth II 16
Empress Matilda 118
EU funds 169
Evolution of Wales exhibition 97, 139
Excavation 35, 115, 117, 149

F

Fisher, George 142
Fitzroy Tavern, London 56
Fortress Baths, Caerleon 117
Foundation stone 16, 36
Fox, Sir Cyril 59, 63, 66
Free entry 160
Friends of the Museum 69, 80, 83
Fron Haul 153

G

Galileo 53
Gallery of Material Culture 98
Geological Survey of Great Britain 39
George III 93
George V 16, 36
Gilbert, Sir Alfred 48
Gilfach Ddu 104
Glamorgan Pottery 73
Glanely Discovery Gallery 150
Goethe, J W 21
Gogh, Vincent van 70
Gregynog Hall 55, 89, 90, 142
Gregynog Press 36, 53, 90, 142
Gulbenkian Prize 156, 169
Gwasg Gregynog 142
Gwendoline & Margaret Davies Charity 142

H

Hallett, Howard Mountjoy 46
Hamilton, Captain Edward 64
Heming, Thomas 93
Henry I 118
Henry VII 80
Heritage Lottery Fund 103, 153, 166, 170
Hermes, Gertrude 142
Historic Buildings Unit 135, 172
Howard Roberts Gallery 129
Hoyle, W. Evans 12, 24

Index

Hughes-Stanton, Blair 142
Hunt, William Holman 26
Hydrozincite 121

I

Impressionist, Impressionism 11, 89, 90, 109, 141
Industrial Revolution 104, 169
Industrial strategy 169
Iron age finds 59

J

Jackson, James Frederick 95
James, John Herbert 53
Jenkins, Evelyn 87
Jenkins, John 44
John, Augustus 56, 70, 83, 89, 90, 109
John, Gwen 56, 109
John, Sir William Goscombe 48, 51
Jones, Hugh R. 103, 107
Jones, Thomas 78
Jurassic fossils 95

K

Katheryn of Berain 80
King Stephen 118

L

Lady Henrietta Somerset 93
Lady Llanover 43
Leatherback turtle 136
Lee, John 44
Leighton, Frederic 48
Lescouezec, Eugénie 141
Lewis, David 125
Lewis, Sir Edward 60
Llanbedrgoch, Anglesey 149
Llanberis 153
Llandeilo 172
Llyn Cerrig Bach 59
Loans Exhibition 19, 55
Lord Leverhulme 109
Lord Pontypridd 4, 8, 36
Lovespoons 74
Lowerison, Bellerby 95
Loyal Address 36

M

Mackworth, Sir Digby 44
MacNamara, Caitlin 56
McCance, William 142
Meissen 23
Melvill, James Cosmo 76
Melvill-Tomlin Collection 76
Merthyr Tydfil 53, 131, 132
Millais, John Everett 26
Moncke, Maria 78
Monet, Claude 70, 89, 141
Moon rock 97
Morisot, Berthe 89
Municipal Museum 8, 11, 15, 16, 30

N

Namuwite 121
Nance, Ernest Morton 73
NASA 97
National Assembly for Wales 142
National Flat Textile Collection 123
National Heritage Memorial Fund 144
National Library of Wales 4
National Museum Cardiff 53, 69, 97, 113, 136, 150
National Roman Legion Museum 44, 117
National Slate Museum 103, 107, 153, 169
National Waterfront Museum 166, 169
National Wool Museum 123, 169
Neanderthals 115
Nicholls, Thomas 51
North, Frederick J. 39, 95, 113

O

Oral history 85
Oriel 1 66, 98
Outreach Service 69

P

Parker, Agnes Miller 142
Peate, Iorwerth 66
Penegoes 40
Penrhyn Strike 103, 104, 153
Pibgorn 43
Piper, John 89, 129
Plant fossils 32
Pontnewydd Caves 115
Portable Antiques Scheme 162, 165, 170
Porthcawl 46
Prefab, prefabricated house 154
Prince Albert 39
Princess Caroline Matilda 93
Ptolemy 53
Pyke Thompson, James 8, 26, 29, 30, 36

R

RAF 29, 59
Reardon Smith, Sir William 36
Re-erection 135
Regeneration award 166
Renoir, Pierre-Auguste 70, 141
Reynolds, Sir Joshua 144
Rhyd-y-car 131, 132, 135
Richards, Ceri 129

Index

Rippon, Robert H. F. 24
Rodin, Auguste 19, 51, 55, 70, 109
Rodrigues 147
Roman leopard cup 162, 165
Rossetti, Dante Gabriel 26, 29, 30
Royal Cambrian Academy 21
Royal Charter 4, 7
Royal Institute for British Architects award 166
Royal opening 36
Ruskin, John 21, 26

S

Sandby, Paul 144
School Service 69
Seal 4, 51
Sense of Place award 103, 169
Seward, Edwin 29
Shells 76, 147
Shepherd, Phil 165
Shoals of Capricorn Programme 147
Siddal, Elizabeth 26
Sisley, Alfred 89, 141
Slade School of Art 56, 109, 127
Snetzler, John 144
Sound Archive 66, 85
South Wales Coalfield 39, 159
South Wales Pottery 73
Spencer, Stanley 89, 129
St Fagans Castle 60, 63, 66
St Fagans National History Museum 51, 66, 98, 131, 135, 154,172
St Michael's Church, Ewenny 11
St Teilo's Church 172
Stone Age 165
Sully 46
Swansea 39, 73, 118, 166

T

Tanygrisiau 153
Tatern, William James 36
The Goldsmiths' Company 170
Thomas, Dylan 56
Thomas, Owen Evan 74
Thomas, Thomas Henry 21
Toilet service 93
Tomlin, John Read le Brockton 12, 76
Tregynon, near Newtown 142
Trevithick, Richard 83, 113
Triple Harp 43
Turner House 26, 29, 30, 36
Turner, Joseph Mallord William 11, 29, 30, 70, 90, 141

U

University of Wales 4, 32, 85, 142

V

Vascular Plant Herbarium 15
Vaynor Collection 53
Vikings 149

W

Wedmore, Sir Frederick 29
Weiss, Marthe 51
Welsh Archaeological Trusts 165
Welsh Assembly Government 16, 160, 169
Welsh Development Agency 169
Welsh Industrial Maritime Museum 110, 113, 169
Welsh Joint Education Committee 69
Welsh National Herbarium 15
Wenallt Hoard 118
Wheeler, Sir Mortimer 35
Wheeler, Tessa 35
Whitehead, Alan 74
Whiteley Spinning Mule 123
Williams, Derek 129
Williams-Wynn, Sir Watkin 64, 93, 144
Wilson, Richard 40, 78, 90, 144
Winton, Wilfred de 23
Wrexham 64, 144, 170
Wright, Thomas 40
Wynnstay Estate 64, 144

Z

Zuccarelli, Francesco 40